1 MONTH OF
FREE
READING

at
www.ForgottenBooks.com

By purchasing this book you are eligible for one month membership to ForgottenBooks.com, giving you unlimited access to our entire collection of over 1,000,000 titles via our web site and mobile apps.

To claim your free month visit:
www.forgottenbooks.com/free669847

* Offer is valid for 45 days from date of purchase. Terms and conditions apply.

ISBN 978-0-267-60086-1
PIBN 10669847

This book is a reproduction of an important historical work. Forgotten Books uses state-of-the-art technology to digitally reconstruct the work, preserving the original format whilst repairing imperfections present in the aged copy. In rare cases, an imperfection in the original, such as a blemish or missing page, may be replicated in our edition. We do, however, repair the vast majority of imperfections successfully; any imperfections that remain are intentionally left to preserve the state of such historical works.

Forgotten Books is a registered trademark of FB &c Ltd.
Copyright © 2018 FB &c Ltd.
FB &c Ltd, Dalton House, 60 Windsor Avenue, London, SW19 2RR.
Company number 08720141. Registered in England and Wales.

For support please visit www.forgottenbooks.com

Eugenics Record Office

BULLETIN No. 7

THE FAMILY-HISTORY BOOK

COMPILED BY

CHARLES B. DAVENPORT

FROM RECORDS AND SCHEDULES FURNISHED BY

GEO. S. AMSDEN, M. D.	**W. M. HEALY, M. D.**
WILLIAM F. BLADES	**AUGUST HOCH, M. D.**
FLORENCE H. DANIELSON	**E. R. JOHNSTONE**
MARY O. DRANGA	**H. H. LAUGHLIN**
W. E. DAVENPORT	**RUTH S. MOXCEY**
A. H. ESTABROOK	**E. B. MUNCEY, M. D.**
H. H. GODDARD	**HELEN T. REEVES**
WINIFRED HATHAWAY	**DAVID F. WEEKS, M. D.**

With sixteen figures in text and
six plates

Cold Spring Harbor, N. Y.
September, 1912

Eugenics Record Office

BULLETIN No. 7

THE FAMILY-HISTORY BOOK

COMPILED BY

CHARLES B. DAVENPORT

FROM RECORDS AND SCHEDULES FURNISHED BY

GEO. S. AMSDEN, M. D.	W. M. HEALY, M. D.
WILLIAM F. BLADES	AUGUST HOCH, M. D.
FLORENCE H. DANIELSON	E. R. JOHNSTONE
MARY O. DRANGA	H. H. LAUGHLIN
W. E. DAVENPORT	RUTH S. MOXCEY
A. H. ESTABROOK	E. B. MUNCEY, M. D.
H. H. GODDARD	HELEN T. REEVES
WINIFRED HATHAWAY	DAVID F. WEEKS, M. D.

With sixteen figures in text and
six plates

Cold Spring Harbor, N. Y.
September, 1912

HQ747

TABLE OF CONTENTS

INTRODUCTION.. 6
I. THE RECORD OF FAMILY TRAITS................................ 7
    Sample Record... 7
II. GENEALOGICAL RECORDS...................................... 13
    a. The Genealogy of the X Family.......................... 14
    b. The History of the Beecher-Foote Family................ 28
III. DATA FURNISHED BY BIOGRAPHIES............................ 36
    Example 1.. 37
    Example 2.. 38
IV. THE RECORD OF SPECIAL TRAITS.............................. 40
V. RECORDS OF RECENT IMMIGRANTS, by Rev. W. E. Davenport...... 46
VI. RECORDS OF NEGRO-WHITE CROSSES, by Florence H. Danielson.. 51
VII. RECORDS OF THE FEEBLE-MINDED AND PAUPERS................. 53
    Family History of Emma H., by Helen T. Reeves............ 53
    The Nam Family—Dr. A. H. Estabrook....................... 58
VIII. RECORDS OF EPILEPSY..................................... 62
    Study of an Epileptic Family.............................. 63
IX. RECORDS OF THE INSANE..................................... 64
    a. Guide to Analysis of Personality—Drs. George S. Amsden and August Hoch... 64
    b. Record of the C Family, with much Insanity, by R. S. Moxcey... 67
    c. Huntington's Chorea, by Dr. Elizabeth B. Muncey............ 73
X. RECORDS OF THE CRIMINALISTIC. Data furnished by Dr. W. M. Healy and Mrs. Mary O. Dranga.. 74
XI. RECORDS OF SEX OFFENSE.................................... 76
    Family History of an Inmate of a Girls' Home, by Mrs. Winifred Hathaway.. 77
XII. THE STUDY OF HUMAN HEREDITY, by Davenport, Goddard, Johnstone, Laughlin and Weeks... 85
    1. The Field Worker...................................... 85
    2. The Chart... 87
    3. The Description....................................... 90
    4. Methods of Analysis................................... 92
    Appendix 1—Forms for written Description of the Chart..... 95
    Plates I–V.. 96
    Synopsis of Abbreviations Adopted......................... 101

INTRODUCTION.

One of the commonest requests made of the Eugenics Record Office by those who are anxious to coöperate in gathering data is for "blank schedules." Some such schedules we have, indeed, provided; but it is impracticable to devise schedules that will meet all requirements. The trained field workers of the Eugenics Record Office are not encouraged to use definite schedules, but to secure data adapted to giving information on the specific points they are studying. They are provided with paper ruled to facilitate the making of charts and writing descriptions in duplicate. The purpose of the present compilation is to show how the various sorts of family histories are prepared. The histories printed here have often been much abbreviated from the original, in order to keep the whole work within desirable limits, but enough is given to illustrate the method of recording Family Histories of the different classes. The figures were prepared by Mr. William F. Blades.

The records are here printed without names, excepting those that are taken from published books. This is in accordance with the agreement made with those who furnish records; namely, that data is held as confidential. "Confidential" means that no names will be published nor the data permitted to be used so as to furnish food for one of the most unfortunate "depraved" appetites that a human being can be cursed with—a love of gossip and scandal-mongering. Data are used for study and analysis and for publication of the results so as to be of scientific and social use. Data may be furnished to students for scientific inquiry, to those contemplating marriage, and even, in some cases, to state officials, to whom organized society has a right to look for the care of its broadest interests. It is hoped that it will in time come to be generally regarded as a social duty to record and deposit in the vault of the Eugenics Record Office data concerning the hereditary traits of one's family.

I. THE RECORD OF FAMILY TRAITS.

Note: The Eugenics Record Office (in combination with the Carnegie Institute of Washington's Department of Experimental Evolution) has issued printed schedules with the above title, of which over 10,000 have been distributed. The person who receives the schedule assigns himself to a place in the pedigree—as father, mother, child, etc.—and places his relatives to corresponding places in the schedule. The commonest error made in filling out the schedule is a curiously egocentric one: under "Father" is given the writer's father; under "Child No. 1" the writer's first child; and the writer and his or her consort nowhere appear. The safest method is to describe oneself first. The value of the Record of Family Traits is, for the Record Office, that it demonstrates the existence of, and locates, the numerous strains with dissimilar traits. Here is a tubercular family, here a family resistant to lung diseases. There is a family of farmers, here of seamen, and so on.

The Eugenics Record Office will send a copy of the blank schedule to any person who will undertake to fill it out and return it. The Office will gladly send a second copy to any collaborator in order that a copy may be kept in the family. It is very desirable that a record of traits should be made as soon as possible; for as the older people die they carry with them many facts of family history that, unless recorded, become lost forever.

The sample Record given is one of a school teacher: pride and sensitiveness derived from the mother's side; with energy, dictatorialness and some artistic talent from the father's side.

SAMPLE RECORD.

FATHER'S FATHER.

J. E. Born Oct. 6, 1805, near Nashville, Tenn.; resided always on the farm where he was born; occupation: school teacher, farmer. In middle age, liable to hemorrhoids; died at 76 of Bright's disease; a good farmer; honest to a dot; did not slight his work; capable and respected; fond of books and a joke; delicate looking, though quite healthy.

FATHER'S MOTHER.

M. C. Born Feb. 1, 1811, near Nashville, Tenn.; resided in Williamson Co., Tenn. (county of her birth); occupation: a farmer's daughter and a farmer's wife. She was never sick a day until she broke her leg at the age of 70. "Her husband never had a doctor's bill for her," was the phrase. Died at 88 years, of senile decay. Industrious, spun, wove, knit well and much, especially after being crippled; very dictatorial, great scold, severe, pious.

MOTHER'S FATHER.

G. M. D. Born ——, near Newark, Ohio; resided in Licking Co., Ohio,—La Salle Co., Ill.,—Sumner Co., Kan. Occupation: farmer. Died at age of 79 of creeping paralysis after la grippe. Never underwent any operations, but had a severe attack of typhoid fever in youth. Proud, anxious to be very wealthy, aristocratic; poor judgment in investments; a great tease; very partisan.

MOTHER'S MOTHER.

K. G. Born ——, near Newark, Ohio; resided in Licking Co., Ohio,—La Salle Co., Ill.,—Sumner Co., Kan. Occupation: farmer's daughter and farmer's wife. Died at the age of 77 of pneumonia. Had erysipelas and her first attack of pneumonia in middle age, but never underwent any operations. Proud, sensitive, good memory, fond of reading, partisan, good cook, affectionate, good nurse.

FATHER (for father's fraternity see below).

J. A. E. B. Oct. 11, 1835, near Nashville, Tennessee. Resided near Nashville and in various towns in Colorado and Illinois; occupation: farm boy, Methodist minister at 53 years. Died at age of 73 of chronic cystitis and prostatitis. Suffered in youth with catarrh of stomach and an attack of typhoid fever. Good speaker and student, good interpretative voice; sensitive, sympathetic, quick-tempered, heavy, well-shaped, vigorously religious, nervous, disliked manual labor.

MOTHER (for mother's fraternity see below).

M. E. D. B. Feb. 4, 1846, near Ottawa, Ill. Resided near Ottawa, in various Tenn., Ill., and Colo. towns. Occupation: farmer's daughter, school teacher, minister's wife. Suffered from prolapsus uteri, overcome when child-bearing ceased. Underwent no operations, but in youth suffered with constipation and ills resulting therefrom; not robust, but not often sick. Good student, teacher, nurse and seamstress; sensitive, proud, fond of music, worries a good deal, nervous.

CHILD NO. 1.

M. K. E. B. March 19, 1879, in Central City, Colorado. Resided in towns in Colo., Ill., Tenn., where father preached longest. Occupatiou: School teacher, farmer's wife. Has undergone no operations, but in youth suffered with sick headache, catarrhal colds, and has had a severe attack of typhoid fever. Fond of books, music, flowers, and farm-work. Likes study; good memory, sensitive, sometimes sulky, lacks self-confidence; called Puritanical.

CHILD NO. 2.

C. B. E. B. Jan. 25, 1881, in Pueblo, Colorado. Has resided in various towns in Ill., Nashville, Tenn., and the longest in De Kalb, Ill. Occupation: School teacher, now critic teacher in the State Normal School. In youth suffered with headaches, hemorrhoids, hoarse colds, nervousness; has had a nervous breakdown, and was operated on for hemorrhoids and for growth in the rectum. Good at all study, especially arithmetic and history; successful teacher, good in music, and with needle. Lacks poise; has good taste and is admired for personality; worries, very nervous, dictatorial.

CHILD NO. 3.

E. C. E. B. —— in De Lehn, Kankakee Co., Ill. Has resided in various towns in Ill., in Nashville, Tenn., Loveland, Colo. Occupation: School teacher and farmer's wife. Suffered with tonsilitis, nightmare, female trouble, constipation, pneumonia, congestion of lungs, measles, very sick in childbirth, nervous breakdown; no operations. Fond of music, good housekeeper, good primary teacher, very sensitive, nervous, dictatorial, sympathetic, affectionate, not strong.

CHILD NO. 4.

G. L. E. B. Sept. 28, 1885, in Nashville, Tenn. Resided in towns in Ill., Tenn., and Colo. Too frail for any occupation. Suffered with sick headaches, catarrh, styes, slipping of knee cap, deafness, nervous breakdown; had grave attack of typhoid fever. Fond of books and music; great tact in care of children, sensitive, nervous, good-tempered, devout, affectionate, sympathetic.

MOTHER'S FRATERNITY.

S. L. D., mother's brother, b. 1840; lives in Walkerville, Montana. Short, medium-brown hair and gray eyes, imperfections of sight only

EUGENICS RECORD OFFICE, BULLETIN NO. 7.

	Father's Father.	Father's Mother.	Mother's Father.	Mother's Mother.	Father.	Mother.	Child No. 1.	" 2.	" 3.	" 4.	" 5.	" 6.	" 7.	" 8.	" 9.	" 10.
SEX OF CHILD. F. Female. M. Male							F	F	F	F						
Age for which description is given							33	31	29	26						
(a.) 10. Adult or present height, inches (no shoes) or v. s. (very short), s. (short), m. (medium), t. (tall), v. t. (very tall).	73	80	70	70	70	66	62	65	67	61						
(a.) 11. Adult or present weight, lbs. or s. (slender), m. (medium). c. (corpulent).	135	200	182	105	190	120	150	120	122	105						
12. Color of hair (before graying) a. (albino, white), f. (flaxen), y-br. (j-brown), l. br. (light brown), m br. (medium brown), d. br. (dark brown), n. (black, nigrum), cl. r. (clear red), d. r. (dark red), d. br. r. (dark red).	n	n	l.br	n	mbr	l.br	y.br	l.br	f	n						
13. Color of eyes. p. bl. (pale blue), d. bl. (dark blue), bl. br. (blue with brown spots), l. br. (light brown), d. br. (dark brown), n. (black), y. bl. (yellow) blue-gray or green), r. br. (reddish brown).	y.bl	p.bl	p.bl	d.br	p.bl	y.bl	p.bl	l.br	p.bl	y.bl						
13a. Note if color differs in the two eyes, dif. or if eyes constantly wander or twitch, tw.																
14. Complexion or skin color bl. (blond), i. (intermediate), br. (brunette) d. br. (dark brown), n. (black, negro), y. (yellow), y. br. (yellow-brown), r. br. (reddish brown).	i	i	bl	br	i	bl	bl	br	bl	br						
15. General mental ability 1. (poor; failure to advance at school). 2.(medium to good). 3. (exceptionally good).	3	3	3	3	3	3	3	3	3	2						
Special ability as below Note: In each ability the grades to be as follows: 1. (poor). 2. (medium to good). 3. (exceptionally good).																
16. In vocal music	2	2	1	1	2	1	2	2	3	1						
17. In drawing or coloring	1	1	1	1	1	1	1	1	1	1						
18. In literary composition	2	2	1	3	2	3	2	3	3	2						
19. In mechanical skill	1	3	2	2	1	2	2	2	2	1						

THE FAMILY-HISTORY BOOK. 11

21. In remembering											
22. General bodily energy 1. (very inactive), 2. (ordinary), 3. (exceptionally energetic)					2	2	2	1			
23. Condition of sight 1. (blind), 2. (imperfect; wears glasses), 3. (strong)					3	2	3	3			
24. Age when sight defect, if any, was acquired or, c. (congenital; born defective)							28				
25. Color blind?											
26. Condition of hearing 1. (deaf), 2. (defective) 3. (strong)			2	3	3	3	3	1			
27. Age when hearing defect, if any, was acquired c. 1 ʰⁱ; brn ᵃᵗᵉ).			45					22			
28. Condition of speech n. (normal), l. (lisping), s. (stammering), d. (dumb); spch ᵗʰᵉ).			n	n	n	n	n	n			
29. Age when speech fect was acquired c. ᵍᵃˡ).											
30. Temperament p. (phlegmatic, slow), i. (intermediate), n. ᵗⁱᵉˢ, quick).			n	i	i	n	n	n			
31. Use of l mds a, ᵂᵂ), l. (left handed), r. (right handed)			r	r	r	r	r	r			
Dets of olflly form as few mak (X) any that may be present. 32. Birthmarks											
33. Hare lip											
34. Abnormal fingers or toes											
35. Dissymmetry of trunk											

☞ Give the data asked for (using figures or letters) in the blank spaces at the right. Enter the data in the proper column for grandparents (columns 1–4), parents (columns 5, 6), and children (columns 7-16).
☞ Fill out lines 25 and 32 to 35 by marking a cross (X) wherever the trait is found.
☞ If more than ten children, use an additional blank.

a The numbers given are illustrative merely.
b Frail health impaired ability to study.

Fig. 1.

due to age; fond of books, affectionate, industrious but slow, proud.

L. D. G., mother's sister, b. 1842 and d. 1906 of cancer. Height above medium, dark-brown hair and eyes; proud, sensitive, good cook, fine looking, fond of reading.

E. B. D., mother's sister, b. 1844 and d. 1910 of cancer. Of medium height, dark-brown hair and eyes; proud, sensitive, moody, good cook, fine looking, fond of reading.

E. B. D., mother's sister, b. in Walkerville, Montana. Of medium height, yellow-brown hair and light-blue eyes, overtired by work; proud, sensitive, good housekeeper, slow, visionary, fond of reading.

C. D. M., mother's sister, b. 1863 in Walkerville, Montana. Height above medium, dark-brown hair, dark-brown eyes, wears glasses; proud, sensitive, fond of books and study, teacher, draws and paints, musical.

L. D., mother's brother, b. 1848 and d. 1902 of pneumonia. Above medium height, dark-brown hair and eyes, wore glasses from age; proud, sensitive, fond of books and study, lacked judgment, fine looking.

F. N. D., mother's brother, b. 1854 in Walkerville, Montana. Short with dark-brown hair and eyes, wears glasses from age. Proud, sensitive, accumulative, fond of reading and likes horses.

C. D., mother's brother, b. 1856 and d. 1897 of pneumonia. Very tall, yellow-brown hair and light-blue eyes; proud, sensitive, fond of reading, silver miner, as were all the other brothers.

E. L. D., mother's brother, b. 1865 in Central City, Colo. Very tall, yellow-brown hair and light-blue eyes; proud, sensitive, fond of reading, good manager of men, affectionate.

FATHER'S FRATERNITY.

H. C. E., father's brother, b. 1829 and d. 1907 of enlargement of liver. Tall, dark-brown hair and light-blue eyes; tyrannical, not over honest in family money affairs, religious, affectionate to his own.

D. C. E., father's brother, b. 1831 and d. 1911 of bladder trouble. Of medium height, dark-brown hair and light-blue eyes; honest, kind, easy-going, industrious, severe if aroused.

J. A. E. P., father's sister, b. 1846 in Nashville, Tenn. Tall, black hair and dark-blue eyes, wears glasses all the time, but only on account of age. Industrious, pious, fine nurse, complains a great deal, good cook, good seamstress.

M. E. S., father's sister, b. 1852 in Nashville, Tenn. Of medium height, light-brown hair and eyes, wears glasses from age; industrious skillful needlewoman, sharp wit, pious, capable.

M. C. E., father's sister, b. 1854 and d. 1899 of tuberculosis. Of medium height, dark-brown hair and blue, short-sighted eyes; cross, industrious, sick a great deal, good singer, pious.

E. E. A., father's sister, b. ——, and d. 1904 of tuberculosis. Of medium height, dark-brown hair and light-brown eyes; had a "cat eye." Industrious, fond of music, pious and capable.

M. E. R., father's sister, b. ——, d. 1885 of tuberculosis. Tall, with dark brown hair; industrious, slow, good singer, pious and lovable.

M. E., father's sister, b. 1852 and died before she was twenty of tuberculosis. Above medium height, light-brown hair, industrious, slow, subject to styes.

B. E., father's sister, b. ——, and d. ——, of tuberculosis.

II. GENEALOGICAL RECORDS.

The purpose of many genealogical records seems to be purely legal; to establish relationships. But many genealogists have a higher aim—to make a record of the life histories of the members of a family. A genealogy conceived in the latter fashion can be of great use in the study of human blood lines, provided the whole truth be told; provided the less as well as the more socially desirable traits be recorded; and that physical traits (including causes of death) be given. The old idea that traits are private and personal things must be done away with, and everyone should feel willing to let it be generally known what combination of traits fell to his lot. In that combination there is ground neither for vanity nor regret.

One great defect mars nearly all genealogies: the defect of following the male line only—the trail of the *name*. However useful our system of following the patronymic alone may be in law and social intercourse, it should not be employed in the genealogy that makes any pretense of providing material for the study of hereditary traits in the past, or of predicting the traits of children. The mother's blood contributes quite as much to the child as the father's; in fact, some traits are inherited by sons only from the mother's side of the house. To be sure, this method of collecting genealogical data would greatly complicate the record. It would be necessary to start with a fraternity, describe the traits of each member of it, pass to the description of the traits of each of the father's and the mother's fraternities with an account of their consorts and offspring. Next take up the fraternities of the four grandparents, their consorts and their children, children's consorts, and children's children. Certain lines might be carried out further to show the source of particular traits or to tie together parts of the network.

We give two sample histories. The first was sent us by a literary man who shows an extraordinary capacity for analyzing his family traits.

1 2 3   4 5   6   7 8 9   11 12   1
 ⌣
twins

III
22 23 24 25
FIG. 2.

a. THE GENEALOGY OF THE X. FAMILY.
♂, male ; ♀, female.

I. 2 ♂. Dissipated, died of some venereal disease early last century.

I. 3 ♂. Tall, black hair, black beard; went to South America late in 18th century; lived there many years; returned to England with a fortune; settled down as a bachelor. Few years later, a native (Indian or Negro) woman, and a group of half-breed children arrived and claimed him as husband and father. He recognized the claim and supported them.

II. 4 ♀. Slender, light-brown hair, blue eyes, deeply religious, patient, strict old-fashioned Quaker, suffered many years with scrofula in the form of a running sore on the leg; born about 1820; died about 1880. Married:

II. 3 ♂. Tall, brown hair and eyes, large Roman nose, deeply religious old-fashioned Quaker, humorous; poor business man; born about 1810; died about 1885.

III. 1 & 2 ♀. Old maids, strict Quakers, tall, dark, slender, passion for flowers and gardening; painted beautifully, intellectual, retiring.

III. 4 ♂. Tall, dark, handsome, Roman nose, fair complexion; manufacturer of patent leather, bankrupt, passion for sport, especially shooting and fishing, painted well. His son and twin daughters (IV, 1, 2, 3) inherit almost all his characteristics.

III. 5 ♂. Very tall, about 6′ 3″, inclined to stoop; had light-brown hair but now very bald, blue eyes, large Roman nose; clever chemist and mechanic; unusually simple in knowledge of the world; nominally a Quaker but fond of getting away from home and having a good time. At age of nearly 70 made ardent love to his nephew's wife; at same time devoted to his wife and family; weak character, easily led; home dominated by wife, who was a woman of a great Quaker family of manufacturers.

III. 7 ♂. Very tall, about 6′ 7″, built in perfect proportion, brown hair, hazel eyes, carried himself well, dressed very well, physieian with large practice, specialist in oculism; wife very nervous little dark woman, died early, leaving one daughter of whom I know nothing (IV, 6).

III. 9 ♀. Tall, slender, graceful, brown hair, hazel eyes; sweet, loving disposition, lost her mind after her husband was fired upon by Land Leaguers in Ireland; was confined in private asylum for a while; more recently at home, mildly insane. Her husband (III, 10) a short, red-haired, blue-eyed irascible Irishman, full of fun, eminent physician, stern father intolerant to vices of his son (IV, 9). The latter, a medical student in Dublin, formed the opium habit; father cast him out; mother visited him in secret in her lucid intervals, and supplied him with money and food. He committed suicide. IV, 8, the latter's brother, a replica of his father in appearance, built up fine practice as surgeon.

III. 11 ♀. Born about 1845; tall, brown hair, hazel eyes, straight nose, sweet temper, loving wife and mother, but just in her reproofs and punishments. Died 1875 of diphtheria when about 30 and enceinte. Painted beautifully, especially flowers. Spent much time in quiet charity. Strict Quaker.

II. 6 ♂. Born about 1801; short, light-brown hair, blue eyes, rosy complexion, Roman nose, very active, successful self-made man, business man, magistrate, mayor of large town in North of England, was called "the Grand Old Man of the North"; stern in justice, almost a crank on neatness of attire, cleanliness of house and person; at 86 recovered from fracture of arm; absolute master in his home and office; Quaker, but not of the strictest type, especially in old age which seemed to modify his earlier rigidity. Had a habit of swinging his stick round and round as he walked. Advised his grandchildren never to worry; said he had never worried in his life, but his sons say trifles worried him, while he took serious matters very philosophically. Had a brother who lived to be 101. Married twice:

II. 5 ♀. Famous blonde beauty. Died young. Only description I have of her is from miniature painted about 1820, which shows her to have reddish-gold hair, blue eyes, oval face, delicate pink and white complexion. Her picture was published in a collection of the famous beauties of England about 1820. Daughter of a prosperous North of England merchant.

II. 7 ♀. (II, 6's second wife) stout, medium height, dark-brown eyes, almost black hair, precise, refined, aristocratic in bearing. Her brother (II, 8) was a domineering English squire, proud, hot-tempered, fond of good wine but not a drunkard, fond of horses, dogs and the society of sporty gentlemen. His daughter (III, 19) was a slender, brown-eyed, dark-haired, irascible woman with hair upon her face; impulsive, passionately fond of her children but accustomed to thrash them unmercifully with a cane for trifling offenses. She inherited her father's fondness for horses.

III. 14 ♂. Medium height, black hair, brown eyes, bald, Roman nose; poor business man, ambitious, active in politics, a magistrate and mayor of North of England city; fond of horses, inclined to display; lived well up to his income. Died suddenly at about 50 of apoplexy. Of his children:

IV. 24 ♀. (Born 1863) is an unmarried woman medium height, slender, dark hair, brown eyes, suggestion of moustache, refined and affectionate, devotes her life to the reclamation of fallen women.

IV. 23 ♂. (Born 1864) died at about 20; was dark blue all over from an imperfect formation of valves of heart.

IV. 22 ♂. (Born 1865) tall, powerfully built, exceptionally hairy, brown eyes, hair and beard. Very strong; went to sea when 14, became a sea captain. Nearly died of yellow fever when about 26: had severe operation for mastoiditis and barely recovered, when between 35 and 40. Married the matron of one of the largest hospitals in London, selecting her largely because of her unconventionality. Was very jealous of her. Became morose, moody, despondent; took to drink; died suddenly at sea when about 40. Left no children. Had been promiscuous in his amours before marriage.

IV. 21 ♀. (Born 1866) is unmarried, small, slender, perfectly formed, oval face, large brown eyes, straight narrow Grecian nose, full lower lip, heavy growth of hair upon cheeks, chin and upper lip, long slender hands; fond of music and dancing, romantic, deeply learned in history, romance and poetry of many nations; principal of one of the most fashionable girls' schools in England. Rides horses splendidly; has suffered severely from spinal neuralgia; afraid of nothing; has seen a ghost several times; it is that of a woman who formerly lived as a king's mistress in the mansion she now occupies; she has tried many times to get this ghost into conversation, but in vain. At the moment of her father's death, though 500 miles away and he had not been ill, she heard him call her as if he was at the door of her room. She took the next train for the city in which he was, and arrived to find he had fallen dead at the very moment she had heard him call. Is idolized by the young ladies who attend her school.

IV. 20 ♂. (Born 1868) medium height, golden curly hair, fair complexion, blue eyes; bad judgment in business and inclined to sharp practice, so much so that relatives will not trust him. Changeable, fickle, ever optimistic, fond of hunting and riding; no idea of living within his income. Married and has several young children to whom he is devoted.

IV. 19 ♂. (Born 1869) short, sturdy build, brown hair and eyes; very matter-of-fact but utterly unconventional and has a vein of the romantic and mystical. Went to sea as a boy; was a rancher in Australia, a surveyor in South Africa, organized the first fire department in Johannesburg; fought in a cavalry regiment throughout the Boer war; almost died of dysentery; returned to Johannesburg after war, and reorganized fire department. Married ignorant farmer's daughter of whom he is very fond; has several children. Cares nothing for refinements or conventionalities. Wonderful story-teller, great imagination, universally beloved.

By his second wife, III, 14 had three children. Mother (III, 13) a nervous woman, full of humor, refined and elegant; grey eyes, brown hair, oval face, prominent front teeth. Of their children, IV, 18 is a brilliant public accountant, short, grey eyes, brown hair, bald at 35, cares little for women's society and still unmarried at 40. Keenly analytical mind; calm judgment; afraid of nothing.

II. 6 ♂. By second wife had three children. III, 20 ♂ (born about 1857) short, brown-haired, grey-eyed, wild as young man; eloped with a barmaid; was clever surgeon and had high reputation as gynecologist. Lost practice through drink. Later did clever work in Egypt exploration under Flinders Petrie; wrote on anthropology. Had no strength of character; ignored his wife's flirtations. She very beautiful, tall, large bust and hips, too slender waist, free and easy in her manners; deserted him and became a harlot in South Africa. Their daughter (IV, 25) was married to a rich man but eloped soon afterwards with an artist, whom she left and returned to her husband.

III. 17 & 18. Are old maids, about 55 and 60 in age. Spend their time travelling about Europe. Can never make up their minds to do anything; fickle, changeable, need someone to "boss" them. Elder has had many flirtations, and could have married one of richest men in England, but was infatuated with his younger brother, a tall handsome sporty fellow who cared nothing for her. Both are intellectual, romantic, refined—almost to excess. Tall, dark-haired, grey-eyed, fair-skinned, oval faces, straight noses.

III. 15 ♀. See also Fig. 3, Gen. B. (Born about 1835) I know nothing about her personally, as she died at the age of about 35, after bearing six children. Her husband, B 1 one of the most successful manufacturers in England, a tall, active, heavily bearded man, born 1826, is still alive. Man of great wealth, little taste but no pretentions to more than he has and glad to take advice of friends in whose judgment he relies. Married three times; children by all wives. I know nothing of children by second and third wives.

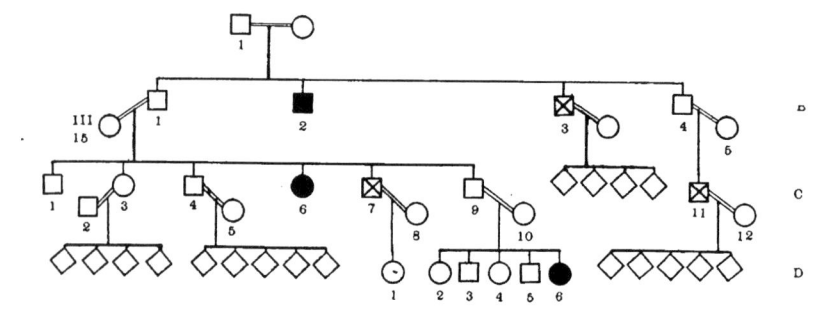

FIG. 3.

B 2 ♂. Harmlessly insane old bachelor. Has to have a companion; generally goes about freely but never alone.

B 4 ♂. (Born about 1825) highly successful manufacturer; great philanthropist; medium height, heavy brown beard, hazel eyes, florid complexion; made a baronet, high principles in business; built and supports an insane asylum; contributes to many charities, spends much time in managing them; active in politics. Wife (B 5) a short, active, intelligent brown-eyed woman, who helps him materially in his charitable work. Their son C 11 clever politician, but unprincipled; seduced the servants in his own house and in those of his friends; wife got a divorce. Has several children, but they are still young.

C 1 ♂. (Born 1855) medium height, grey eyes, slender, light-brown hair, elegant dresser; artist of fair ability, bachelor.

C 4 ♂. (Born 1859) medium height, grey eyes, sandy curly hair; dandy in dress; clever business man, now at head of one of biggest manufacturing businesses in England. Happily married and has several young children.

C 3 ♀. (Born 1854) tall, graceful blonde, grey eyes; happily married and has several children.

C 6 ♀. (Born 1860) insane from birth; had impediment in speech; died at about 40 in an asylum.

C 7 ♂. (Born 1864) thin, medium height, cold grey eyes; narrow, thin nose; quiet but full of sarcastic humor. Careless in dress to the point of eccentricity. Though very rich, goes about in frayed garments. Wife (C 8) had to look after him like a nurse. He was always considered "queer," but is a fairly successful business man of the shrewd sort. Divorced his wife for adultery on her part. They have one daughter.

C 9 ♂. (Born 1866) about 5' 10" high; inclined to stoutness; blue eyes, sandy hair; slight impediment in speech; seduced working girl when about 20, married her, came to America, with practically nothing; made great success as public accountant, acquiring a very large income unaided by his millionaire father. Pillar of the Episcopal Church; president of young men's club. Wife, C 10, born about 1868 about 5' 9"; stout, rosy cheeks, light-brown hair, grey eyes, full lips. Though uneducated, has adapted herself to her husband's position, and takes leading part in society of a great city. Their children are all under 20. D 2, born 1892, is the image of her mother, quiet, refined, musical. D 3 & 5, born 1894 and 1896, the images of their father. D 6, born 1898, insane from birth; in a private insane asylum.

III. 12 ♂. (Fig. 1) born 1846; about 5′ 5″ tall; slight but wiry; red hair, became bald when about 25; hazel eyes inclining to green; active to the point of nervousness. Has had palpitation of the heart. Passion for Alpine climbing and gardening. Fine business man; his word as good as his bond and worries much over trifles. Good artist; no ear for music; eloquent orator; deep student of literature; keenly critical taste in art. Has traveled all over the world; cares nothing for city life; loves long walks where wide views can be had, but hates walking for any distances through woods. Never idle for an instant, and the sight of anyone else idling irritates him. Hot-tempered, but rigidly just. Affectionate, but inclined to repress all manifestations of affection. Charitable, but does all such work in secret; inclined to be close at driving a bargain, and loathes anything savoring of extravagance; generous father and devoted husband. Twice married. Of his children:

IV. 15 ♂. Born 1865; 5′ 10½″ high; slight, hazel eyes inclining to green, fair complexion, brown hair, yellow moustache, reddish beard, hairy; failed at everything he undertook until he by chance drifted into journalism. At this he made fair but not brilliant success. Myopic. Deeply interested in art, literature, science; brought up a Quaker, but became a Roman Catholic at age of 22. Impressionable, poor business man; inclined to extravagance. Susceptible to women, but devoted to wife and family. Intolerant of anything suggesting untidiness or slovenliness; irritated and depressed by trifles, but soon recovers as he is highly, even recklessly, optimistic. In youth was considered the image of his mother (III, 11), but is now, in face, the image of his father (III, 12) though much taller. Easily led; great gourmet but small eater. Conscientious, but inclined to be conceited. (See Fig. 4 for his descendants.)

IV. 14 ♀. (Born 1866) 5′ 9″; the image of her mother, (III, 11); wavy brown hair, hazel eyes, musical, artistic, fond of admiration, mean in financial affairs; married a man she did not love; has had many flirtations since—two at least of which almost resulted in separation from her husband. Has no children, owing to some internal obstruction which an operation failed to remove.

IV. 13 ♂. (Born 1868) 5′ 9″; sallow, thin, brown hair, hazel eyes. Martyr to liver. Gourmet, artistic and musical; deep student of literature; spends all spare money on books. Generous and liberal, sceptical and cynical in matters of religion. Expert tea-taster, but has little interest in business. Bachelor.

IV. 12 ♂. (Born 1873) 5' 5"; stockily built; dark-brown hair; hazel eyes, large Roman nose. Unsuccessful in all business undertakings; fine artist in a mechanical line. Careless about personal appearance; perfectly contented with love in a cottage. Married a girl in humble but respectable position; has one baby.

IV. 11 ♀. (Born 1874) tall, reddish-brown hair; hazel eyes, straight nose, careless about dress, easy-going, deeply religious; married an Asiatic missionary. Oriental life has suited her lazy, sweet disposition. Had some uterine trouble as her older sister had, but a slight operation overcame it. Has one son, 10 years old; typical Oriental type. Has had two or three miscarriages recently; has a baby girl born alive.

III. 12 ♂. Married a second time a widow with three children, all of whom died of tuberculosis, as their father had done. By her, he has one daughter (IV, 10) (placed in diagram between 15 & 16) who is tall, with reddish hair, blue eyes, straight nose, pink and white complexion. She is fickle, but stubborn in love affairs; has many sweethearts, each of whom for the time was the "only man in the world." Romantic, impressionable, good musician, fine singer. Her mother was tall, dark, brown eyes, clear complexion, musical, good singer. Ever since daughter's birth, has been neurasthenic invalid.

IV. 10 ♀. Has been married five years, but has no children.

F 3 ♂. Scotchman, born about 1820, (mother English) 6 feet tall, blue eyes, light-brown hair, which he kept to the day of his death at about 82. Florid complexion; bigoted Presbyterian; scrupulously honest and unselfish, even quixotically so. Poor business man. Failed in business early in life, did better working in positions of trust for others. Uncompromising in his loves and hates. Strict but affectionate father. Hated all sham and everything that tended toward display or fast living. His brother, (F 2), I know nothing of, but the latter's son, now about 70 years old, is a distinguished judge, a lecturer on law in a great university; a man about 6 feet tall, large blue eyes, florid complexion, brown hair; has an affection of the eyes that exposes the inside of the lids. Women say that when he is talking to one, he gives her the impression that she is the only woman he ever loved. Have been several scandals about his relationship with women, but his wife has always shown her faith in, or loyalty to, him by making friends of the women about whom there was gossip. His four sons are distinguished in their professions, two as lawyers, two as engineers. The four sons are married and have young children.

22   EUGENICS RECORD OFFICE, BULLETIN NO. 7.

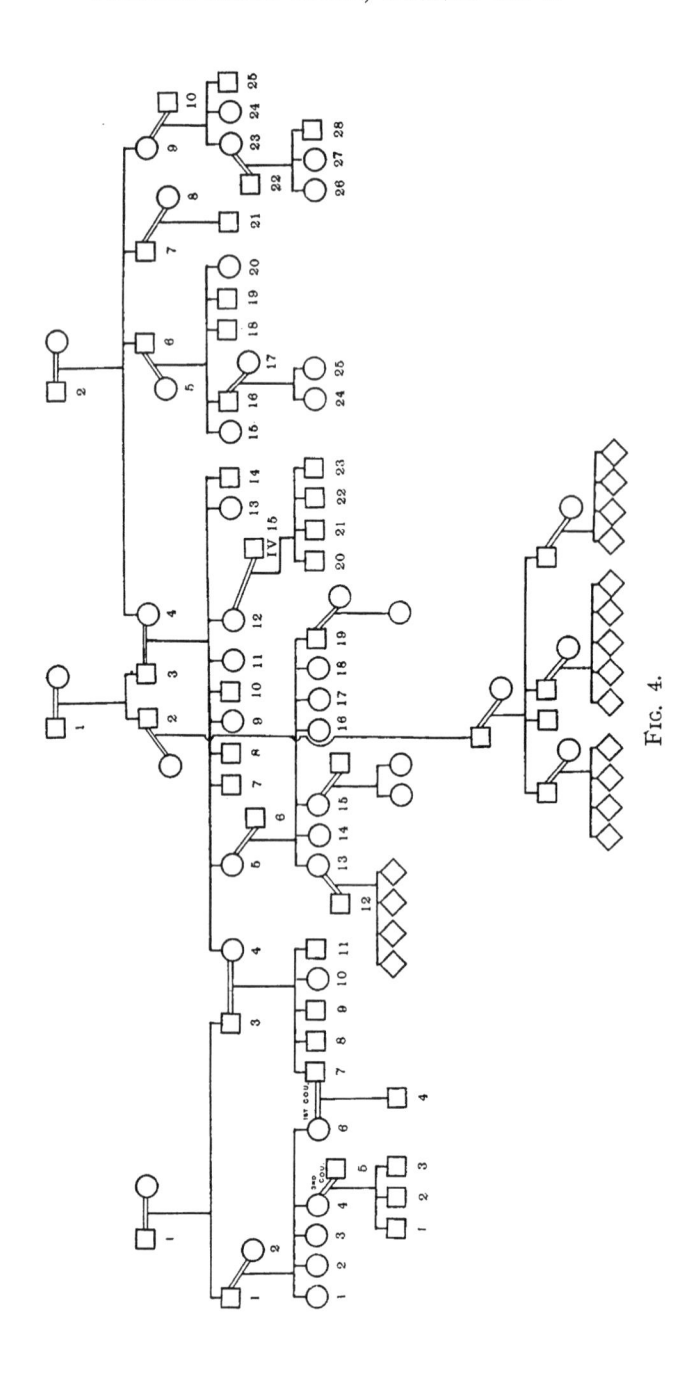

FIG. 4.

F 4 ♀. Born 1829; died 1910 of diabetes; 5′ 10″ tall, hazel eyes, long pointed nose, firm mouth, oval face, fine figure, soft white skin. Brought up a Roman Catholic, but after marriage became Scotch Presbyterian of most bigoted type. Fine business woman. Proud as Satan. After her husband's failure, she managed to bring up her large family in a small country town surrounded by Indians, and miners, like ladies and gentlemen, preventing them from associating with other children. On moving to large city, took her place at once in its most exclusive society. Contrived to save about $10,000 out of her husband's slender salary, which she invested little by little in gilt edged stock. Fought for her rights in the courts even when this involved breaks with old friends. Hospitable to a fault; house always full of indigent friends, always open to relatives at all hours. Could not see a joke, but made some of the cleverest jokes herself. Her father, E 2, colonel in British army, married an Englishwoman. Her brother:

F 6 ♂. One of the most famous surgeons on this continent. Born about 1830; died about 1906 of acute gastritis. About 6 feet tall; long pointed nose; grey eyes; mouth a straight line; proud, full of humor; an aristrocrat to the marrow; the idol of the poor in his city; had a vast practice; lectured on surgery in several great universities; spoke several languages; travelled extensively; was at various times elected to high office in city and country; knighted by Queen Victoria, and by Pope Leo XIII. Married late in life. Brought up a Presbyterian, he became a Roman Catholic; gave liberally to Catholic charities; was lavishly generous but with poor judgment; would slip a $10 gold piece into the hand of a 6-year-old nephew whose parents were well off, but forgot entirely nephews and nieces whose parents were obliged to struggle to keep things going. Careless about business matters, and thoughtless in his management of the estates of poorer relatives. In important lawsuit entrusted his case to young lawyer just graduated, simply because youth needed the money; lost the case through lawyer's bungling, but did not care. Of his children, G 18 ♂ is a Jesuit priest, tall, thin, pointed nose, thin lips, weak-looking eyes, eloquent, deep student. G 16 ♂ is about 30 years old, tall, blue eyes, blonde, pointed nose, thin lips, a rising surgeon. Married and has two blue-eyed blonde babies. Other children young or dead.

F 7 ♂. Short, dark-grey eyes, long pointed nose; married an intensely religious shrew; liked to escape and have a quiet good time with the boys. Had an only son, tall round face, short thick nose, blue eyes, thin lips. This young man (G 21) is musical, fond of companions beneath his station in life, simple in tastes, commonplace in every way. Married a woman who went to the bad; remarried a working woman who died. Has no children by either.

F 9 ♀. Short, stout, light-brown hair, many oddly-shaped moles on back covered with fine hair; blue eyes; a crank on auction sales; bought every useless thing that seemed cheap. Frittered away a fortune. Lavish entertainer; impulsively generous and did not hesitate to impose upon friends in like manner. Know nothing of her husband. Of their children, G 25 ♂, born about 1852, unmarried, very religious, childishly simple in tastes, loves theaters and good eating; keen sense of humor, but cannot make a joke or tell a story. G 24 ♀, born about 1857, unmarried, fond of gayety, frivolity and flirting. Has grey eyes, exceptionally large bust, thick curly hair. G 23 ♀, born about 1858, is married to very rich man; leader of society in large city; lavish entertainer; myopic, has gone blind in one eye, and other is almost blind; about 50 years old; short, slender; light-brown hair; hazel eyes. All those three have long bodies and very short lip. G 22 ♂ has had three children; boy died of typhoid fever, two girls are musical and intellectual; care nothing for society, but only for art and literature and music.

G 4 ♀. Born about 1855; tall, reddish blonde hair; blue eyes; complexion like apple blossom; graceful figure; died of tuberculosis at age of about 30. Her husband, G 3, short, volatile Frenchman, proud, lazy, alcoholic, too proud to work, neglected his family after wife's death, and allowed his children to be brought up by their maternal grandmother. Of these, H 7 ♂, born about 1878, medium height, curly red hair, blue eyes, industrious, temperate, easily led by those he loves; has made success in business, though starting with nothing. Married H 6 ♀, his first cousin. She is a tall, vivacious brunette, dark-brown eyes, rosy cheeks, fine figure; she is the "boss." They have one child, a boy about 6 years old, delicate, golden hair, blue eyes. H 8 ♂, born about 1876, ran away; he had no home, and after cruising around many places, married a German servant. They have some children. He is a tall, red-haired, blue-eyed man who cares nothing but for home and simple comfort. H 9 ♂, born about 1877, stocky, dark red hair, hazel eyes; generous, self-sacrificing; hard worker; eloped with another man's wife, old enough to be his mother, she deserting several children. They have several children. H 10 ♀, born about 1879, medium height, red hair, bright light-blue eyes, yellow lashes, freckled face, slender graceful figure, has a faculty of making herself useful to others; adaptable, self-sacrificing, foolish about money matters, inclined to be impulsively extravagant, has earned her own living, is about (Jan. 1912) to marry a man two years her junior, an only son of very rich and aristocratic parents.

H 11 ♂. Born about 1880, medium height, red hair, freckled, grey eyes. Has wanderlust; ran away from school often as child, robbed his aunt, when 13; fired from a school for stealing a watch; an inveterate liar, but a genial, pleasant, loveable companion.

G 5 ♀. Born about 1852; medium height, very stout, dark-brown hair, brown eyes, long pointed nose, easy going, full of fun, a fine cook and a good housekeeper. Her husband a conceited boaster, but a clever engineer, was for long a drunkard, but at the age of about 60, he gave up liquor absolutely. She has always been kind, long-suffering and gentle with him, and never has hinted to anyone that he was not the best husband in the world. Their children are all the images of their father, but have most of their mother's characteristics. H 13, married to a clergyman who was basely untrue to her, was loyal to him and effected his reform.

G 7 ♂. Very tall, dark brown hair and beard; long pointed nose; died of tuberculosis at about 30, complicated with some venereal disease.

G 8 ♂. Very tall, brown hair, brown eyes, musical, full of humor, great story teller, fond of yachting, swimming and all sports. Died of tuberculosis and rheumatism at about 30.

G 9 ♀. Born about 1850; short, square-jawed, grey eyes, long pointed nose, large mouth, one leg shorter than the other; never married. One of the most self-sacrificing women in the world; spends all her life trying to find things to do for others and doing them.

G 11 ♀. Born about 1852; short, slender, brown eyes, large mouth, big teeth, one white lock in brown hair, tender hearted, sentimental, hot-tempered, cries whenever she says goodbye even for a day. Has had several love affairs, but never married. Full of fun; passionately fond of her nephews and nieces whom she spoils terribly. Timid to a ridiculous degree.

G 12 ♀. (Born abt. 1860) 5' 10" tall; perfect figure, soft white skin, hazel eyes, dark brown hair; long pointed nose; small mouth, narrow jaws, oval face, small chalky teeth; suffered from rheumatism as a girl; had severe attack of typhoid fever at age of 48; suffered severely from malaria when 30—35. Affectionate, devoted to family;

demonstrative in love for her children when babies, but gradually less so as they grow older; finds it difficult to make any demonstrations of affection for husband or grown up sons; but would sacrifice her health and her life for them. Hard worker but utterly without any idea of system. No sense of locality or direction. Bad memory for names. Fond of music, cares nothing for literature or art; more conscientious than religious, though inclined to bigotry; intolerant and uncharitable in her judgments of others; inclined to worry. Proud of family; would lie or kill to protect any of them; utterly lacking in curiosity; married at 30 and had not the faintest idea of what marriage meant or whence babies came. Of her and (IV, 15's) children, H 20 ♂, born 1891, is 6' 2" tall, hazel eyes, brown hair, sallow complexion, nervous, optimistic, abnormally narrow upper jaw but large teeth, had to have upper jaw stretched; has suffered much from inflammatory rheumatism and tonsilitis; adenoids removed when about 15. Had scarlet fever and measles when a small child. Had malaria when 2 years old. Physically powerful, muscular, but inclined to stoop. Passion for mechanics and electricity; studied the theory of these as a boy; thoroughly mastered them before he was 18. Would not study at school, failed in high school; but is making a fine success in the employ of a great electrical manufacturing concern. Got into serious trouble when 15 by trying to seduce girl of 13; since then has cared little for girls' society, acting as if afraid of them. Hates "society," but has a few warm friends, generally in a station of life rather beneath him. Careless about personal appearance, fidgety, contracts little habits of fidgeting with trifles; on the go all the time. Affectionate, thoughtful, unselfish, and considerate of others, but fickle in his friendships, rushing them at first, then suddenly forgetting them. On his holidays, prefers a farmhouse to a fashionable resort. Keen sense of humor; tells a story well until he comes to the point, when he laughs so hard that he cannot finish it intelligently, or has to repeat it when his laugh is over.

H 21 ♂. Born 1893; 6' tall, thin but broadchested and muscular; fearless, strong constitution. As a child of 2 to 4, enjoyed nothing better than getting into a cold bath with the thermometer at zero, and the window wide open; did it with impunity. Dived off into ten feet of water, trusting to someone to catch him when a child of 2. Learned to swim when very young, and to-day, will swim for hours as far out at sea as he can get. At six learned to box and would put on the gloves with his father and take all the punishment the latter could give, without losing his temper. Good football player. As a boy cared for nothing but sport. Always careful about associates; would never make friends with people beneath him. At 18, knows all the nicest girls in the city in which he lives, and is a prime favorite with them. Straight nose, brown eyes, brown hair, the face of a Greek god; large strong teeth, but inclined to be chalky; very hairy legs and body; at 18 had to shave regularly. Hard to move, stubborn, determined to have his own way, very thoughtless of others; a dandy in dress. Persistent and patient in attaining his end in spite of all obstacles. Diligent worker when once started, and whatever he does, he does thoroughly. Wears scarcely any underclothing in coldest weather, and sleeps with little over him. Has never had any disease except measles when a baby.

H 22 ♂. Born 1896; 5′ 9″ tall; well built; brown hair, large strong teeth, yellowish hazel eyes, Roman nose, plump rosy face, hot petulant temper, quick student and diligent. Loves outdoor sport and mechanical pursuits. Always had a weak stomach, but eats greedily, and it is hard to make him chew his food. Is often laid up with fever and sore throat, due to overeating or greediness in eating rich food, but a day's starvation cures him.

H 23 ♂. Born 1905; always large for his age; grey eyes, rosy cheeks, light brown hair that is red in the sunlight; never sick. Powerful imagination; plays by himself, making of himself an entire football or baseball team. Loves outdoor life. Remarkable musical taste; picked up piano-playing without aid and has such a good ear for music that he can find correct chords and harmonies alone.

G 1 ♂. Born about 1850; a Frenchman of medium height, dark brown hair and eyes, large nose; dissipated but religious. Never able to support family, but always able to live well himself, and associate with the best people. Clever engineer, but cannot hold a position because he will not take orders from anyone. Married G 2 a slender, refined, half-French, half-Irish girl; large blue eyes, wavy golden hair, Roman nose, small mouth, oval face. She was a famous beauty in the South, but has become through worry, a nervous and physical wreck at 60, and looks 90. Very religious, strict Roman Catholic, intolerant, sarcastic, bitter and not altogether sincere. Brought up her five daughters, all of them rare beauties, under great difficulties, but made refined and elegant ladies of them. They are all of same physical type, tall, well-built, rosy-cheeks, brown eyes, large straight nose with large nostrils, perfectly-shaped mouths, and slender hands; all inclined to display, and extravagant in dress. H 6 married her first cousin, already described. H 4 ♀ is selfish, silly in money matters, no idea of economy, discontented, melancholy, says she was born sad and is always sadder when the sun shines; married a rich man she did not love; he was a dark, black-eyed, short man of French-Italian parentage, a successful, self-made business man, her third cousin. Of her three children, I 1 ♂ was born 1906 with a pyloric obstruction and died in 30 days; I 2 ♂ was born 1907 with a pyloric obstruction which was cured, and today he is a robust, fat, black-eyed, curly haired, active, hot-tempered boy. I 3 ♂, born 1910, with a hare lip, and absolutely no palate; the bone that carries the upper incisors is also absent. Operation closed the lip and made a nostril. 1912 is cutting teeth; second incisors are growing at edge of jaw bone on brink of opening. Lower teeth coming normally. He has red hair, blue eyes; physically robust, trying hard to talk.

b. THE HISTORY OF THE BEECHER-FOOTE FAMILY.

Every family that comprises genius that is commonly regarded as of high order offers points of great interest. In how far is the genius sui generis? Whence came the strain of large imagination? Is this imagination associated with eccentricity and flightiness such as we see in the insane?

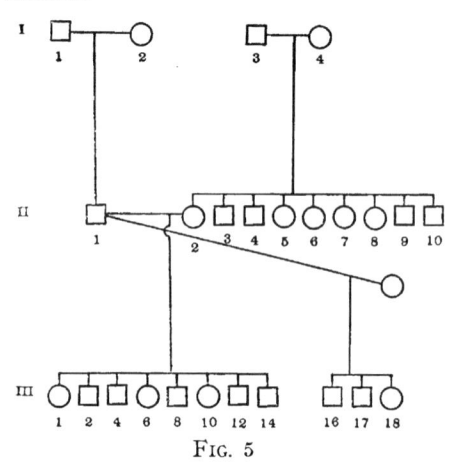

FIG. 5

As an example we select the "Beecher family"—a family that includes two persons of "Hall of Fame" grade: Henry Ward Beecher and Harriet Beecher Stowe, his sister.

III. 1. Catherine Esther Beecher, b. E. Hampton, L. I., Sept. 6, 1800; d. Elmira, N. Y., May 12, 1878. Educated at Litchfield, Sem., Conn. She prepared her own text books in arithmetic, theology and mental and moral philosophy. In 1832 went to Cincinnati with her father and started a seminary there, but her health failed. She then devoted herself to plan for the physical, social, intellectual and moral education of women, which was promoted through a National Board of Popular Education, that sent hundreds of women as teachers into the south and west. Her mind was full of original vigor, but without much imagination, consequently some of her schemes were impracticable. She had a great deal of racy humor, and mother-wit, with patience, magnanimity, and unbounded good-nature, no bitterness or malice; while working for women's education she opposed woman suffrage and college education for them. Her own common sense was her standard of judgment. She believed that what she could not comprehend could not exist; had no appreciation of art or classical music; she sang and played the piano and the guitar and occasionally wrote verses; for many years she suffered from lameness and weakness of nerve and body; and all her work was carried on under great bodily difficulties. Her published works include "Letters on the Difficulties of Religion," "The Moral Instructor," "Treatise on Domestic Economy," "Housekeepers' Receipt Book," "Duty of American Women to their Country," "Physiology and Calisthenics," "Common Sense Applied to Religion."

III. 2. Rev. Wm. Henry, b. E. Hampton, L. I., Jan. 15, 1802. Educated at home and in Andover. 1833 received honorary degree of A. M. from Yale. Home missionary on the Western Reserve and since held charges in Putnam, Toledo, and Chillicothe, Ohio, in Reading and N. Brookfield, Mass.

III. 4. Rev. Edward, b. Hampton, L. I., Aug. 27, 1803. Graduated at Yale 1822, studied theology at Andover and New Haven; tutor at Yale 1825. Pastor of Park St. Church, Boston 1826-30; president of Ill. College, Jacksonville, 1844; Pastor Salem St. Church, Boston and in Galesburg, Ill. till 1870. Prof. of exegesis in Chicago Theol. Sem. 1872 retired from the ministry. Was senior editor of the Congregationalist for its first 6 years and was constant contributor to periodicals. His two works on the "Ages" gave rise to much discussion, and have modified doctrinal statements as to the origin of human depravity. Married Isabella P. Jones, Oct. 27, 1829.

III. 6. Mary Foote (Beecher) b. July 19, 1805; m. Nov. 7, 1827, Thomas Clapp Perkins of Hartford, Conn., b. July 30, 1798; d. Oct. 11, 1870.

III. 8. Rev. George Beecher, b. East Hampton, L. I., May 6, 1809; d. Chillicothe, Ohio; m. July 13, 1837, Sarah P. Buckingham of Putnam, Ohio. He studied in Hartford under the care of his brother Edward and took a collegiate course at Yale; attended Theol. Seminary at New Haven. His collegiate and professional courses were interrupted by ill health. Had strong social sympathy and a habit of transmitting thoughts and feelings to friends or relatives by letters. He says: "When I am in a weak state of body, unless I have friends with whom I can converse and thus become excited by the collision of intellect, I cannot raise myself to the point of writing with ease." His sermons written under intense excitement. Liked exciting labor, rather than patient, laborious study. Guileless, affectionate, honest, precipitous, broad-minded non-sectarian. Musical ability, as he had charge of two singing schools and often led his own choir. Passionately fond of flowers, shells and other natural objects with beautiful form and color. Interested in total abstinence. He suffered much from dyspepsia, and was frequently depressed in spirits. He was much troubled with weakness of the throat and lungs. In his pastorate he is described as active and ardent; never uninteresting, sometimes surpassingly powerful, but not always happy in his efforts. Died at Chillicothe, Ohio, July 1, 1843, of a self-inflicted gunshot wound.

III. 10. Harriet (Elizabeth) Beecher, b. Litchfield, June 14, 1811. Left motherless at 4 years. Went to aunt's house; committed to memory a wonderful assortment of hymns, poems and scriptural passages; had a very retentive memory and used it later in life. "With the ability to read," Mrs. Stowe said in after years, "there seemed to germinate in me the intense literary longing that belonged to me from that time." From 4 to 6, sought for books: read Arabian Nights at 6. Harriet is described by her step-mother as amiable, affectionate, and very bright. As a girl, on hearing the Declaration of Independence read: "The heroic element was strong in me . . . and it made me long to do something; I knew not what, to fight for my country, or to make some declaration on my own account." At 10 or 11, at Litchfield Acad.: A great joy to be allowed to write compositions. Wrote one that she read at 12 years and father proud of it. Subject: "Can the Immortality of the Soul be Proved by the Light of Nature?" At 12, she went to a Hartford school, and began a drama called Cleon (a great lord at the time of Nero), remarkable for a girl of her age. "Converted" at 14 years. Had an excitable poetic nature. Was subject to hypochondria. "You don't know how wretched I feel, so useless, so weak, so destitute of all energy." In 1832 wrote a geography (pub. 1833). Published a satirical essay in the Western Magazine. Married Calvin E. Stowe, Jan. 1836. Twins, autumn 1838. Literary work while housekeeping, 1840. June 16, 1845: "I suffer with sensible distress in the brain . . . a distress which some days takes from me all power of planning or executing anything." 1850, "When I have a headache and feel sick as I do to-day." The scene of death of her "Uncle Tom" presented itself almost as a tangible vision to her mind while sitting at the communion table; was almost overcome with it and could scarcely restrain the convulsion of tears and sobbings that shook her frame. Love of fun; absentminded. "Mrs. Stowe's face like that of all her mother's children showed the delicate refinement of the Foote mask overlaid by the stronger and more sanguine Beecher characteristics. Curly, crispy hair, eyes kind and pleasant, frame slender with 'scholar's stoop' of the shoulder. Manner self-possessed, gentle, considerate, without the graces of one habituated to society, she was evidently a gentlewoman born and bred." Mrs. Stowe's genius was essentially dramatic. Her own theater, herself among the actors, the scenery never out of her brain. Mind bubbling and boiling; "Think of so many stories that I don't settle on any." Her public readings were a great success! She died July 1, 1896, at 85 years of age at Hartford, Conn. Mind had deteriorated in late years. "Mind almost ceased to act" for some years before her death. (Like her father's) "My mind wanders like a murmuring brook."

III. 12. Rev. Henry Ward Beecher, Brooklyn, N. Y., b. June 24, 1813; d. Mar. 8, 1887; m. Aug. 3, 1837, Eunice White Bullard, West Sutton, Mass. A graduate of Amherst College, 1834; studied at Lane Theological Seminary, 1834-7. Pastorates in Laurenceburg, Ind.; Indianapolis, Ind.; and Brooklyn, N. Y. Editor of N. Y. Independent in 1861, and in 1870, editor of the Christian Union (now the Outlook). He published numerous books. Had great literary and oratorical ability, great personal magnetism. In temperament he was always hopeful, expectant and progressive. Naturally shy and bashful, ran away from his sister's party as a boy and at 60 years confessed that he never entered, without embarrassment, a room in which he expected to find strangers. Witty and quick in repartee, an excellent mimic, usually the center of a circle of tempestuous merriment. In boyhood was a daring leader and desired to excel in everything. Had a habit of investigation and was a close observer. Had a positive genius for friendship. His generosity, fairness, love for his enemies and his self-control, impressed one friend most. He was not an original thinker, but had great philosophical insight, spiritual vision and the power of persuasion in public capacity; in both civil war and reconstruction period, he exhibited prophetic and statesmanlike qualities. He employed the resources of wide reading, broad sympathy with men, vivid imagination and a devout emotional nature. He never could handle figures correctly but saw the philosophy and poetry which underlay mathematics and even statistics. Was rather careless in money matters. Had a great love of flowers, gems, and natural beauty in form and color. He died of cerebral hemorrhage, March 8, 1887.

III. 14. Rev. Charles Beecher, b. Litchfield, Conn., Oct. 7, 1815. Graduated at Bowdoin 1834. Theol. course in Lane Seminary, Ohio. Ordained pastor of 2nd Presbyterian Church, Fort Wayne, 1851, when he went to Newark for three years. 1857 at First Congregational Church, Georgetown, Mass. 1870-77 resided in Florida where for 2 years he was state supt. of public instruction and later pastor at Wysox, Pa. Was an excellent musician, and selected and arranged much of the music for the "Plymouth Collection." Published: The Incarnation or Pictures of the Virgin and Her Son; David and His Throne; Pen Pictures of the Bible; Autobiography and Correspondence of Lyman Beecher. He married Sarah Coffin.

HALF BROTHERS AND SISTERS.

III. 16. Rev. Thomas Kennicut Beecher, son of Harriet (Porter) Beecher, b. Feb, 10, 1824. Graduated from Ill. College 1843 when his brother Edward was president. Pastor of N. E. Cong. Church, in Williamsburg, now Brooklyn, N. Y. and had charge of the Indedendent Cong. Church. Was an influential speaker and writer and is distinguished for philanthropy. Ignores sectarian feelings and seeks to promote a fraternal spirit among the various Christian denominations. Edited a weekly Miscellany in two Elmira papers on current topics. A lecturer; has pronounced mechanical and scientific tastes and is a lover of art as well as a keen critic. Has travelled in England, France, South America and California.

III. 17. Rev. James Chaplin Beecher, b. Boston, Jan. 8, 1828; d. Elmira, N. Y., Aug. 25, 1886. Graduated at Dartmouth and studied at Andover. Until 1861 was chaplain of the Seamen's Bethel in Canton and Hong Kong, China. In Civil War was chaplain and then

Lieut. Col. and mustered out in 1866 as brevet brigadier general. Later held pastorates in Oswego, Poughkeepsie and Brooklyn, N. Y. After 3 years of acute suffering from hallucinations which had been present since 1864, he committed suicide.

III. 18. Isabella Beecher, b. Feb. 22, 1822, at Cincinnati, married John Hooker; she combined many traits of a gifted family. Was an active champion of the claim of women to the ballot.

The parents of the fraternity III, 1-14 were Rev. Lyman Beecher and Roxanna Foote who were married in Sept. 19, 1797.

FATHER.

II. 1. Lyman Beecher, born at New Haven, Conn., Oct. 12, 1775. The only child of David Beecher and Esther Lyman, his wife. He was a 7 months child, weighed scarcely 3 pounds at birth and his mother died of tuberculosis two days after he was born. He was laid aside as not viable, but after awhile, as he continued to breathe, was washed, dressed, and cared for. He grew up in his uncle's family at Guilford, Conn.; worked at blacksmith's shop and farm; placed in a good school where he proved to be the best reader in the school. Graduated from Yale 1797; ordained 1798 and preached in Presbyterian church in East Hampton, Long Island, 1798-1810. In Congregational Church, Litchfield, Conn., 1810-26; in Boston 1826-32; at Cincinnati, 1833-43 and was president of the newly established Lane Theological Seminary at Cincinnati, 1832-50 and professor emeritus until his death at Brooklyn, in 1863. He was tried for heresy, a mark of breath of view in theological matters. Published Views in Theology,1836; A Plea for the West,1835; Sermons on Temperance, etc. Was married three times, first to Roxanna Foote, Sept. 19, 1797, who died 1818; then to Harriet Porter of Portland, Me. His mental traits were as follows: His imagination was apparently visionary (for his behavior was erratic) and suggestive; his memory was retentive; his methods of work on the whole unsystematic, impulsive. He had a love of music and was very susceptible to its influence. He had a piano sent from New Haven to Litchfield, learned to accompany it with the violin, while his sons, William and Edward, played the flute. He had a strong sense of humor and his household was full of cheerfulness and much hilarity, he loved pranks and jokes. He loved fishing and took much vigorous exercise, sawed wood, shoveled sand and lived much in the open air. Seldom wore an overcoat or gloves, nor carried an umbrella, except in extreme cases. He never had property nor sought to acquire it, nor could he keep it if he had it. He had great personal courage. Thus when, at college, he caught a sneak-thief in the depth of the night he brought him to his room, made him lie on the floor until morning and then took him before a judge. He had no fear of, but loved, a thunder storm. But he was impressionable, for when told as a child by a playmate that a fiction he had invented would incur the wrath of God and cause him to be burned forever, he was deeply affected. He knew periods of depression as well as elation. He was displeased at the publication of the private diaries of great men, especially if they were of a melancholy cast or recorded great alternations of ecstasy and gloom. He "had dark hours in his early life, and was able to impart hope to the despondent." He loved action; said, "I was made for action. The Lord drove me; but I was ever ready. I have always been going at full speed." He loved human sympathy and had no words of uncharitableness, envy or jealousy. He was a great correspondent and his children showed the same trait and maintained for years a sort of circulating letter or "round robin." Enthusiastic himself, he inspired this trait in others; thus the arduous work of building up the family woodpile became a rivalry among the children. In his own work he required a mental stimulus to writing; if he had a sermon to prepare, he would talk with the neighbors up to the last moment and then rush to his study and draw up his outlines. In the pulpit he was bold to the point of audacity, and displayed great personal magnetism and an indomitable will. He preferred speaking from notes but was a careful writer. He was a reformer, a controversationalist, a temperance reformer, an optimist, liberal and progressive, but fearful of radical reform, and was extremely absentminded. His physical health was not robust, though maintained by vigorous exercise. He suffered from dyspepsia and in the last ten years of his life was mentally enfeebled.

MOTHER.

II. 2. Roxanna (Foote) Beecher, Guilford, Conn., b. 1775—d. 1818. Daughter of Eli Foote and Roxanna (Ward) Foote. She was easily first in his fraternity of nine in intellect and goodness. She acquired the equivalent of a college education, besides the usual domestic tasks of girls of her time. She read literature and history and science; wrote and spoke French, was skilled in music, art and dressmaking. She was so sensitive and of so great natural timidity that she never spoke in company or before strangers without blushing, and in later life was absolutely unable to lead devotions in the weekly female prayer meetings. Her family were Tories, an indication of character which is so marked a feature in her descendants. She early learned patience, self-control, efficiency and unselfishness. She never spoke an angry word, was submissive, not demonstrative, but with a profound philosophical nature, a depth of affection and a serenity that was charming. She had a love of the beautiful and the poetic temperament which Henry Ward Beecher had. She loved nature, especially flowers. Loyalty came from the Foote family, shown by the anti-slavery stand of her children; virtue and temperance came from the Ward family.

MOTHER'S FRATERNITY.

II. 3. Andrew Ward Foote, b. Nov. 9, 1776; d. Sept. 29, 1794.

II. 4. William Henry Foote, b. Sept. 8, 1778; d. Oct. 7, 1794.

These two boys died of dysentery the same year. They were youths of great promise.

II. 5. Harriet Foote, b. July 28, 1773; d. Apr. 19, 1842. Lyman Beecher says of her in comparing her with her sister Roxanna, whom he married, that she was "smart and witty, a little too keen." II, 6. Martha Foote, b. Sept. 23, 1781; d. Sept. 23, 1793; II, 7. Catherine Foote, b. Feb. 28, 1792 and d. Aug. 27, 1811. II, 8. Mary Ward Foote Hubbard.

II. 9. Samuel Edmund Foote (b. Oct. 29, 1787 and d. Nov. 1, 1858 in New Haven) was a sea captain at 18 years, a profession for which he had prepared himself by study and practice. Abandoned the sea in 1826. Resided in Cincinnati where he did much for the improvement and growth of the city. Was secretary and director to the City Water Company, and a director of the Ohio River Canal and other enterprises. Lost a fortune in the financial crisis of 1837 but gathered another and retired to New Haven in 1850. He was an adventurous spirit, and loved the roving life of a seaman. He was ingenious and invented improvements in ships' rigging and building and this trait made him useful in his public enterprises. He had great practical common sense and business ability united with large ideality. He was a man of wide interests and culture—"one of the best-educated men of his time." He spoke and wrote the French, Italian and Spanish languages fluently; and he had a wide knowledge of literature. He was generous and had a humorous combativeness that led him to attack the special theories and prejudices of his friends, sometimes prosily, and sometimes in earnest. He married, Sept. 9, 1827, Elizabeth Betts, Elliott, a distant cousin.

II. 10. Geo. Augustus Foote, Guilford, Conn. b. Dec. 9, 1789; d. Sept. 5, 1878; m. May 24, 1829, Elizabeth Spencer, b. Mar. 23, 1812; d. Aug. 29, 1898, daughter of Samuel and Elizabeth (Tuttle) Spencer.

GRANDPARENTS.

I. 1. David Beecher, a blacksmith, who worked at the same anvil his father had before him and on same old stump of the oak tree under which John Davenport preached his first sermon in New Haven. He was well read, clear-headed, with decided opinions upon questions of the day. He kept college students as boarders in order to enjoy their conversation. He was fond of politics, loved to keep pets, and was subject to hypochondriacal attacks. He was absent-minded; would collect eggs into his pocket and sit down on them. He was short in stature, like his mother, and like his father and grand-father could lift a barrel of cider and carry it into the cellar, but his grandfather, John Beecher, the immigrant, could lift so as to drink out of the bunghole. David's father was Nathaniel Beecher, six feet tall and a blacksmith, and his mother was Sarah Sperry, a woman of great piety. David's father's father was John Beecher, whose wife was a Pomeroy, a family that includes much talent in blacksmithing, iron-making and inventiveness.

I. 2. Esther Lyman, born Middletown, Conn. daughter of John Lyman, had a joyous, sparkling, hopeful temperament; was tall, well proportioned and dignified in movements. She died of tuberculosis 2 days after her son Lyman was born.

I. 3. Eli Foote, Guilford, Conn. and (I, 4) Roxanna (Ward) Foote. He was a man of fine person, polished manners and cultivated taste. He was educated for the bar and practiced a little in Guilford but eventually became a merchant and traded at the South. He was a descendant of Nathaniel Foote whose family in England had received a coat of arms with an oak tree upon it and the motto, "Loyalty and Truth" for concealing the King in an oak tree in time of danger.

III. DATA FURNISHED BY BIOGRAPHIES.

Many well-written biographies devote space to a valuable account of the "ancestry" of the person described. It is not unusual to find in such accounts evidence of the origin of the combination of traits that made their possessor successful.

EXAMPLE 1.

SUBJECT.

Lyman Abbott, b. Roxbury, Mass. Dec. 18, 1835, graduated from University of the City of New York, admitted to the bar, 1856, ordained to the Congregational ministry 1860; in literary work, 1869-88; pastor of Plymouth Church, Brooklyn, 1888-99. Author of books on law, religion, the Bible, democracy, etc. Editor of the Outlook. Characterized by industry, clearness, and simplicity of exposition; clear thinking and judgment (leading to successful prediction in social affairs), modesty, and much musical ability.

SUBJECT'S FRATERNITY.

Benjamin Vaughan Abbott, graduate of Harvard Law School, secretary of New York Code Commission, 1863-5: reviser of U. S. statutes, (16 vols) digests, etc. altogether exceeding 100 volumes. D. at 59 years, 1890. Much musical ability.

Austin Abbott, b. Boston 1831; graduated from Univ. of City of New York, 1851, practised law with Benjamin Vaughan; prepared greater part of Abbott's New York Digest and "Abbott's Forms." Wrote many other highly practical books to simplify legal procedure. Dean of Law School. Died, 1896.

Edward Abbott, b. Farmington, Me., 1841; graduated from Univ. of City of New York, 1860, and Andover Theological Seminary 1862; on U. S. Sanitary Commission, Army of the Potomac; associate editor of "The Congregationalist," 1869-1878. Joined the Protestant Episcopal denomination and had charge of St. James parish, Cambridge. Published numerous works.

FATHER.

Jacob Abbott, b. Hallowell, Maine, 1803; graduate of Bowdoin college, 1820; studied at Andover Theological Seminary 1821-24; Professor of mathematics and natural philosophy in Amherst College, 1821-24; founded young ladies' school in Boston, preached there and with his brothers founded Abbott's Institute in New York City. D. in Maine, 1879. He was a prolific writer of juvenile stories, brief histories and biographies and religious books for the general reader, and a few works in popular science. His Rollo Books (28 vols.) were enormously popular and he issued over 200 books in all. His chief characteristics were a remarkable judgment, modesty and fondness for little children.

FATHER'S FRATERNITY.

John Stevens Cabot Abbott, b. Brunswick, Maine, 1805. Associated with Jacob in management of Abbott's Institute and in preparing his brief historical biographies. Graduated from Bowdoin College, 1825; preached at various places in Massachusetts. Wrote voluminously books on Christian ethics and history. His historical works were popular but not scholarly. Rose early and worked two hours before breakfast; an assiduous student who consulted nature as much as his library. Visualized his histories before writing. Was never discomposed nor in a hurry. Died Fair Haven, Conn. 1877. (Nat. Cyclopedia, VI; 145.)

Gorham Dummer Abbott, b. Brunswick, Me., Sept. 3, 1807. Graduated Bowdoin College, 1826; studied theology at Andover; took horseback ride through South for his health. Established, with his brother Jacob, the Mount Vernon School for Young Ladies and became, 1837, pastor of Presbyterian Church at New Rochelle. Collected and tabulated data on the educational facilities, institutional methods and systems of instruction, libraries and publications for the use of schools in this and foreign countries. Organized (1836), and for some years served as secretary of, the "Society for the Diffusion of Useful Knowledge," which published selected books for school libraries. Secured useful legislation for public education. Founded private academies; was interested in studies in biblical exegesis, in history and in problems of commerce and political relations with Central America and Mexico. Died So. Natick, Aug. 4, 1874.

Samuel Phillips Abbott, founded in 1844, at Farmington, Maine, the Abbott school, popularly called "Little Blue"; a teacher and a lover of youth. Two sisters and one other brother.

FATHER'S FATHER.

——————— ————, very musical.

MOTHER.

Harriet Vaughan, musical.

EXAMPLE 2.*

SUBJECT.

George Bancroft, b. Oct. 3, 1800 at Worcester, Mass. As a boy called "wild." Early schooling meagre, then at Exeter Academy where

---

* M. A. deWolfe Howe: "Life and Letters of George Bancroft," Scribner, 1908.

he showed traits of intellectual quickness and ambition and won (1813) the prize for best classical composition. Then at Harvard College where he bore the nickname of "The Doctor," and was elected to the Phi Beta Kappa society. Studied in Europe, 1818-1822, at Heidelberg, Göttingen and Berlin. Taught at Harvard, and later organized a secondary school for boys, 1822-31. Married Miss Dwight of Springfield, Mass. Entered political life, nominated for Governor of Massachusetts, 1844, became Secretary of the Navy under Polk, 1846, became influential in annexation of Texas and the settling of the Northwest boundary dispute. Minister to London in 1846; to Berlin, 1867; recognized as leader in diplomatic circles, died at Washington, 1891. His great literary work is his History of the United States, begun 1836, of which five volumes appeared. His work characterized by a philosophic spirit, as well as by accuracy. He had great imagination and enthusiasm, capable of large generalizations. Said of him that he had two principal faults: Getting excited over little things, and having little respect for the judgment ot others.

SUBJECT'S FRATERNITY.

Lucretia Bancroft, married William Farnum.

Jane Putnam Bancroft, mother of Admiral Gherardi.

Henry Bancroft, a sea captain in the East India trade and sailing master of one of McDonough's vessels in the battle of Lake Champlain. Died at 30 years.

John Bancroft, followed the sea and was lost at sea at 32 years.

Eliza Bancroft, married "Honest John" Davis, former governor of Massachusetss and a U. S. Senator.

FATHER.

Aaron Bancroft, born at Reading, Massachusetts, Nov. 10, 1775; died at Worcester, Massachusetts, August 19, 1835. Entered Harvard College 1774, graduated with honor, 1778; given degree of D. D., 1810. On leaving college taught unsuccessfully, then went to Nova Scotia to preach. Rebelled against Calvinism and became a Unitarian; was indifferent to praise or fault finding; was president of the Unitarian association, 1825-1826; wrote in 1807 a "Life of Washington," which brought him fame.

A bright, cheerful and hospitable man who loved the society of intellectual friends; had a ready sympathy, was lively in conversation, quick and clear in perception. His mind was calm, logical, reflective, he loved literature and its pursuits. Temperament bilious, physical organization delicate, irascible in boyhood, but later self-restrained. Affection strong, but not demonstrative. Died four months after his wife.

FATHER'S FATHER.

Deacon Samuel Bancroft.

FATHER'S FATHER'S FATHER.

Deacon Thomas Bancroft of Reading, Mass. He left a will reciting: "My history books to be divided among my three sons equally," etc. (showing his interest in history.)

MOTHER.

Lucretia Chandler; "of remarkable benevolence, had uncommon gifts of mind, playfulness and cheerfulness." As a child "cared not for history nor did I read much of travels." Read many novels, liked plays and blank verse. Always ready for amusements; the gayness of the ball room; called "black-eyed Indian."

MOTHER'S MOTHER.

Mary Church of Bristol, R. I. whose father's father was Captain Benjamin Church of King Philip's War, and a chronicler of the Indian Wars.

MOTHER'S FATHER.

John Chandler, filled various offices of importance in the provincial government of Massachusetts. Came of a family conspicuous for wealth and social place. Known as "Tory John"; fled to Halifax at the opening of the Revolution.

IV. THE RECORD OF SPECIAL TRAITS.

Almost every family has one or more interesting inheritable traits, which can be traced through two or more generations, and a record of which will be of great value. The Eugenics Record Office issues small blank schedules for the recording of such data. One of these is reproduced below. The first line is for the name and address of the person responsible for filling out the schedule. The second is for the name and trait of some person in the family who serves as a starting point in the description and is called "subject." The third line is for the subject's address, in order that further details may be inquired into.

Name of Collaborator B. M—
Full Name of Subject W. J. W—
Present Address A— M—

Full Description of Trait in Subject red hair

GIVE BELOW THE NUMBER OF RELATIVES THAT HAVE THE SAME TRAIT AS SUBJECT (PRES) AND THE NUMBER WITHOUT IT (ABS)

TRAIT	Pres	Abs	TRAIT	Pres	Abs	TRAIT	Pres	Abs	TRAIT	Pres	Abs
1. Father	X		5. Father's Father	X		9. Mother's Father		?	13. 2d Cousins, Father's Side	1	0
2. Mother	X		6. Father's Mother	X		10. Mother's Mother		?	14. Own Cousins, Mother's Side		
3. Brothers	1	0	7. Father's Brothers			11. Mother's Brothers		—	15. Brother's Children		
4. Sisters	2	0	8. Father's Sisters			12. Mother's Sisters		—	16. Sister's Children		
									17. Wife (or Husband) if any		
									18. Consort's Ancestors		
									19. Consort's Collaterals		
									20. Own Children (if any)		

DESCRIPTION OF RELATIVES HAVING THE SAME TRAIT AS SUBJECT.

RELATION-SHIP (NO.)	NAME	ADDRESS	DESCRIPTION
1	J. W—	A— M—	red hair
2	Nellie C—	do	red hair
3	Elmo W—	do	} red hair
	Jean W—		
4	Lerna W—	do	red hair
13	Robert M—	do	red hair

Note here if parents or consort (if married) are consanguineous; and degree
(OVER)

IF MORE SPACE IS NEEDED USE A SECOND BLANK.

Address A—, M—
Town and State A—, M
Date June 1, 1912

FIG. 6.

EUGENICS RECORD OFFICE.

This blank is for the use of PHYSICIANS, TEACHERS, SOCIAL WORKERS, PARENTS and others in studies upon the inheritance of various interesting traits. Addresses are asked for in order that, if there is no objection, further inquiries may be made.

Several blanks may be used for a family with cross reference from one blank to the other.

☞ **ALL DATA WILL BE HELD AS STRICTLY CONFIDENTIAL, AND NO NAMES WILL BE PUBLISHED.**

The blanks filled out should be mailed to: EUGENICS RECORD OFFICE, COLD SPRING HARBOR, N. Y., Blanks for full FAMILY RECORDS furnished free on application.

DESCRIPTION: The earliest generation is at the top of chart, the youngest at bottom. Short vertical lines suspend symbols of the members of a fraternity from the long horizontal fraternity line. Short horizontal or oblique lines connect consorts. Symbols that represent individuals described on the other side of this sheet to be shaded.

SAMPLE GENEALOGICAL TABLE

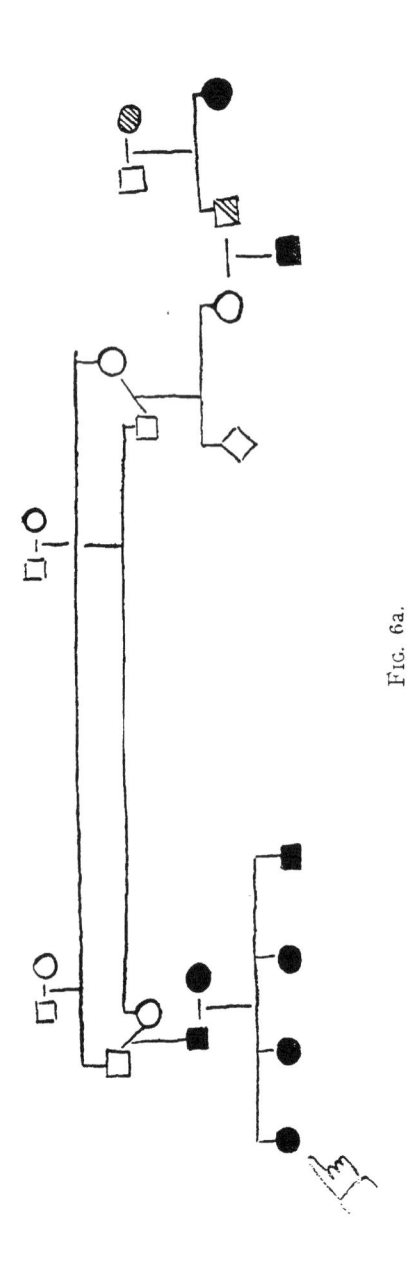

SPACE BELOW FOR A GENEALOGICAL TABLE, PREPARED LIKE SAMPLE ABOVE ▯,—MALES; ○,—FEMALES

FIG. 6a.

Name of Collaborator Henry O. Marple, M.D. Address 2246 Michigan Av.

Full Name of Subject William J. Henderson   Town and State Milwaukee, Wisc.

Present Address 17 Broad St., Lincoln, Nebr.   Date July 28, 1912

Full Description of Trait in Subject Hare lip which is not extreme but suffi-
cient to require a surgical operation.

TRAIT	Pres	Abs	TRAIT	Pres	Abs	TRAIT	Pres	Abs
1. Father	X		5. Father's Father	X		9. Mother's Father		
2. Mother	X		6. Father's Mother	X		10. Mother's Mother	X	
3. Brothers	1	0	7. Father's Brothers	0	5	11. Mother's Brothers		5
4. Sisters	0	3	8. Father's Sisters	3	2	12. Mother's Sisters		2
						13. Own Cousins, Father's Side	1	8
						14a. Moth. moth's niece Own Cousins, Mother's Side	3	
						15. Brother's Children	1	
						16. Sister's Children		
						17. Wife (or Husband) if any		
						18. Consort's Ancestors		
						19. Consort's Collaterals		
						20. Own Children (if any)	2	

DESCRIPTION OF RELATIVES HAVING THE SAME TRAIT AS SUBJECT.

RELATION-SHIP (NO.)	NAME	ADDRESS	DESCRIPTION
3	A. H——	17 Broad St., Lincoln, Nebr.	hare lip and cleft palate, recently mar.
5	B. H——	Fairview, Oxford Co., Ohio	scar on lip, repaired hare lip?
13a	C. I——	dead	hare lip, died young
14a	D. K——	dead	hare lip

Note here if parents or consort (if married) are consanguineous; and degree

(OVER)

IF MORE SPACE IS NEEDED USE A SECOND BLANK.

FIG. 7.

EUGENICS RECORD OFFICE.

This blank is for the use of Physicians, Teachers, Social Workers, Parents and others in studies upon the inheritance of various interesting traits. Addresses are asked for in order that, if there is no objection, further inquiries may be made.

Several blanks may be used for a family with cross reference from one blank to the other

☞ **ALL DATA WILL BE HELD AS STRICTLY CONFIDENTIAL, AND NO NAMES WILL BE PUBLISHED.**

The blanks filled out should be mailed to: Eugenics Record Office, Cold Spring Harbor, N. Y., Blanks for full Family Records furnished free on application.

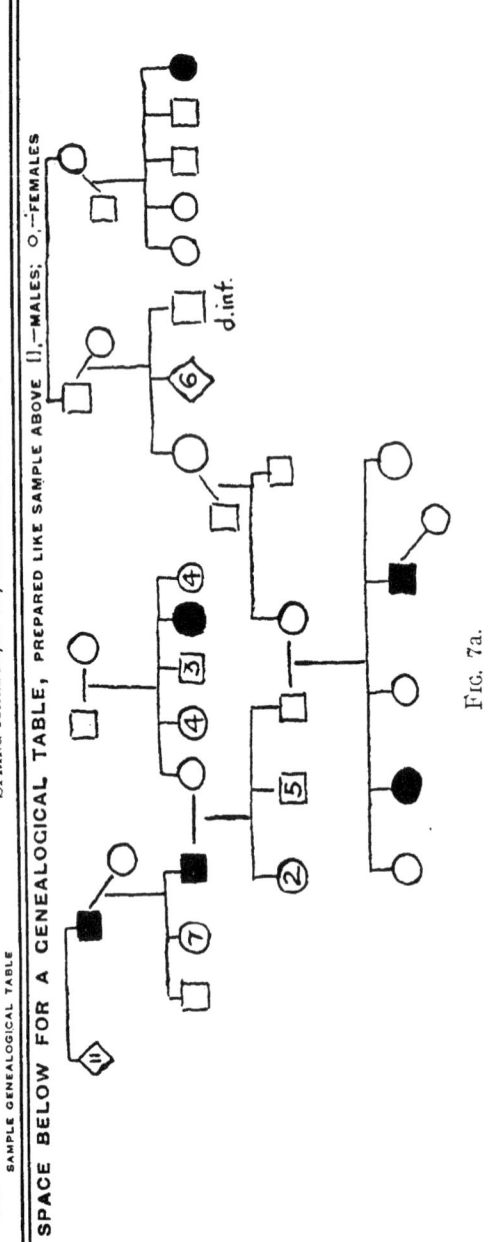

DESCRIPTION: The earliest generation is at the top of chart, the youngest at bottom. Short vertical lines suspend symbols of the members of a fraternity from the long horizontal fraternity line. Short horizontal or oblique lines connect consorts. Symbols that represent individuals described on the other side of this sheet to be shaded

SAMPLE GENEALOGICAL TABLE

SPACE BELOW FOR A GENEALOGICAL TABLE, PREPARED LIKE SAMPLE ABOVE ▯.—MALES; ○.—FEMALES

Fig. 7a.

The fourth and fifth lines are for a brief record of the inheritable trait as it occurs in the subject. The middle of this face of the schedule is devoted to a statistical summary of the distribution of the trait in the relatives of the subject; each relative or class of relatives is numbered for reference to the descriptions in the lower part of the schedule. Where there are two affected brothers, they may be designated as 3a, 3b, and so on. In 3, 4, 7, 8, 11 to 20 give the number of the persons who have the same trait as the subject and the number who lack it. In the lower part of the schedule is given the name and address of the relatives who have the same trait as the subject and a brief description of the trait as it occurs in them. The last lines ask for information as to consanguinity.

The obverse of the schedule is for a genealogical chart which shall set forth the precise relationships of the members of the family—the "subject" being designated by an index ☞. In the chart, squares indicate male individuals, circles females. Symbols for brothers and sisters are suspended from the same horizontal line. Consorts (i. e. wives or husbands) are connected by means of single (or double) oblique lines, preferably single. Any fraternity is connected with its parents by a short vertical line. Individuals who bear the same trait may be represented by solid black symbols; those who show the trait, but less marked, by shaded symbols. Teachers have a great opportunity in securing records of special traits.

In the first example given (Figs. 6 and 6a), we have in the upper (first) generation two pairs of parents—each the parents of two children; the son of one of these parents married the daughter of the other pair; and the daughter of the first, the son of the second. The first couple had a son with the trait in question, and he married a similar. Their four children had the trait. The second couple had only two children of whom the older (the daughter) married a man with the trait slightly marked, whose mother was like himself, but had a daughter with the trait well marked. The son of this pair had the trait.

In the second example (Figs. 7 and 7a) we have in the first generation four pairs of parents three of which are parents of persons with hare lip. In the second generation one parent has hare lip and the other parent has an affected sister; while of the second pair of parents one is known to have a first cousin with hare lip. Then a generation is skipped, followed by the last generation with two out of five in the fraternity who have hare lip.

V. RECORDS OF RECENT IMMIGRANTS.

The stream of immigrants, often amounting to thousands in one day, that enters this country constitutes a great problem, inasmuch as the probable nature of their germ plasm—the condition of their progeny—is unknown. Nor will an inspection of the body of the immigrant enable us to decide whether he or she will produce socially desirable offspring. There is only one reasonable way to keep up our social standards, and that is to exclude immigrants who obviously belong to bad strains. Such strains can be detected best by studies made at the country of emigration.

To enforce the importance of "blood" and family traits it is desirable to study the families of recent immigrants who have arrived in America during the great immigration that began in 1880 and has not yet ceased. As a sort of model of such studies, of which we ought to have hundreds, we reproduce a report by Rev. W. E. Davenport, Head Worker at the Italian Settlement, Brooklyn, N. Y.

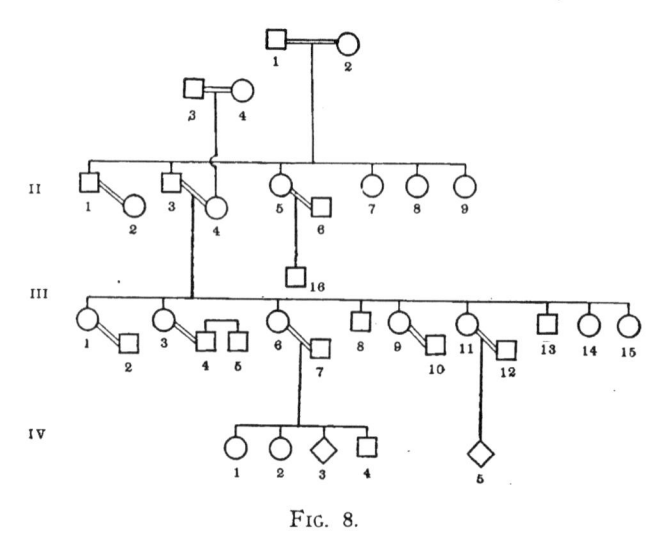

FIG. 8.

THE A—— FAMILY, FROM SICILY.

Thirteen years ago, Rosario A—— (II, 3, Fig. 8), born 1856, pursued in Bagheria near Palermo, Sicily, his deceased father's trade of cooper. He was tall, strong, muscular and active, and had, a few years before, weighed over two hundred pounds; but he suffered occasionally from early rupture. His hair and eyes were black, his complexion swarthy, his forehead low and square, and his features regular.

Economically he was successful. He lived in his own two-storied house, the lower part of which contained a wine-press and cooperage shop. He made and sold much wine every Fall, employing at the vintage season four or five men; he also made casks and barrels. Seven years earlier he had bought a lemon orchard for 10,000 lire, hoping that the income from it would help maintain his family. He never saw army service, and was illiterate.

His blue-eyed father (I, 1) died of shock, a sudden injury, eight years before, aged 65. His strong, well-preserved, devoted mother (I, 2), 70 years old, looked to him for support. His only brother (II, 1) had married, and moved to Palermo, where he prospered in the dry-goods business. Of his four sisters, all married, two were in fairly prosperous circumstances. One, Pauline (II, 5), born 1852, is short and strong, has dark eyes and dark hair, a broad forehead and regular features. She married Leonardo P. but after she was 50 years old, she left him and came to Brooklyn (1905) to live with a married son who was a longshoreman.

In 1877, Rosario A—— married Guiseppina C—— (II, 4), of medium height, fair complexion, brown hair and eyes. She is fond of jewelry, vain of her plain looks, superstitious, prone to gossip about her neighbors, shiftless and careless of her daily duties, and with an unruly temper. Her father (I, 3), a clerk, died young; her blue-eyed mother (I, 4) died of cholera in 1873.

By 1898, Rosario had met with business reverses. Owing to the ravages of the Phylloxera, the wine crops for two years had failed, and the dowry of 5,000 lire that he had given his eldest daughter (III, 1) on her marriage had depleted his purse; so he came with his eldest son (III, 8) to Brooklyn to improve his fortune. He quickly found work in Arbuckle's cooperage, and about a year later his son did likewise. Then, in 1899 his second daughter (III, 3) was sent for to help keep the rooms and earn wages in a factory. Finally, in 1902, with good work and thrift, Rosario was able to send for his wife and other children except the married daughter. They arrived Feb. 23, 1903. Three months later Rosario was taken to the Brooklyn Hospital, suffering from hernia and intestinal stricture, and was operated upon successfully. But, despite the doctor's warning, he returned to work too soon, his trouble recurred in a severe form, and he died, December 1903. With the aid of her second daughter, his wife retained her apartment and brought up her unmarried children. Stomach trouble developed in 1903, diagnosed first as a tumor and, in 1905, as cancer. Despite a weak heart, she worked in a factory intermittently to make up her rent; but, throughout 1910, she failed rapidly, attended by a nurse from the Bureau of Charities, and died the same year.

Of the children of Rosario and Guiseppina, the eldest is Guiseppina (III, 1), born 1878 near Palermo, and still living there. She is of medium height and has brown hair and blue eyes and regular features. Her husband, Nicolo R—— (III, 2), who has simplex brown eyes, was, at the time of their marriage, and *is,* a thrifty raiser of and dealer in lemons. The second child is Francesca (III, 3), born 1884. She is of medium stature, has chestnut hair and eyes, a lighter complexion, and regular features, and is very illiterate. Since her marriage in 1902 to John L—— (III, 4), she had tubercular cysts removed from her neck and chest. John L—— reached Brooklyn in 1896, from Ponticella, near Bagheria. He is strong, of medium height, has a swarthy complexion and coal-black eyes. He is illiterate but energetic, honest and affectionate. Brought up in Italy as a fisherman, he here first worked on the docks; in 1901 he started to peddle fish with a basket license, and later, like his brother Sebastino III, 5, (who is also married and lives on Hudson Avenue, Brooklyn) he opened a fish store. He improved financially, but in 1908, he was struck by a falling cask on the docks, where he occasionally worked, and went to the hospital with both collarbones broken. In 1911, he secured damages in the sum of $1,000, of which all but $450 went to lawyers and witnesses. From March 1911 he and his family have maintained a small fish store on Atlantic Avenue, paying $53.00 rent per month, and doing an unsatisfactory business.

The third child of Rosario and Guiseppina is Concetta (III, 6), b. 1888, a fairly strong young woman of medium height, brown hair and eyes, fair complexion, and regular features except that the lower jaw protrudes somewhat. She is industrious and particularly neat and increasingly tasteful in the care and decoration of her rooms. She suffered in 1905 from throat trouble and "nervousness" which she has since overcome. From 1902 until her marriage in 1906 she was employed in Gair's box factory. She married Alfonso A—— (III, 7), b. 1889 in Cefalu. He is large-bodied, strong, has wavy brown hair and brown eyes and a full face; has good sexual habits, likes music, is socially inclined and an active member of an Italia-American political club. He is loyal but superstitious and lacking in initiative.

reflection and mental force. He was convicted, in 1906, for taking a sack of iron rivets from the yard of the company where he was employed. A month's imprisonment strengthened a naturally good inclination, or served as an efficient deterrent, but he is still liable in some things to "lose his head." Suffers from hernia and has periodical attacks of tonsilitis probably aggravated by the poisonous fumes in the paint factory where he has been employed for the past four years. He earns $12.00 per week on which he maintains his family, paying $12.00 per month for rent. His father, Salvatore, is a tall, heavily-built, gross-featured man with large hands, and curly black hair. He ran a marionette theatre in 1901-3; bears a bad reputation and left for Baltimore in 1900, under charge for betrayal of girls, both in Italy and America. His wife remained in Brooklyn, living with a married daughter. The children of Concetta and Alfonso are: Antoinette (IV, 1), b. 1907, heavy, fair, curly brown hair, chestnut eyes, broad face and forehead. Salvatore (IV, 2), b. 1908, of stocky build, fair skin, curly flaxen hair and broad forehead; infant, b. 1909 and died; Rosario (IV, 4), b. 1911.

The fourth child of Rosario and Guiseppina is John (III, 8), b. 1887, who came to America with his father in 1898. He is tall, with blue eyes, chestnut hair, light complexion and of neat and attractive appearance. He is deficient in reflection, resolution and mental force. He likes reading in both English and Italian, and plays the guitar. He has had bad sexual habits from boyhood, suffered in 1903 from pleurisy, nervous trouble and lung weakness, but recuperated in consequence of a summer in the country. Began factory work in 1900, entered Arbuckle's sugar house in 1905, and worked there for a year. Then was attacked by pneumonia, typhoid, and venereal disease and sent to Cumberland Street Hospital where valvular disease of the heart developed. Returned to Italy August, 1906, where he lived with his oldest sister one year. Returning to Brooklyn, 1907, he first re-entered the factory, but as he suffered from persistent heart weakness and venereal trouble, he was unable to continue such heavy work, and became a barber, in which occupation he earns five to seven dollars a week, and lives in a rented room with his married sister whom he pays $2.25 per month rent. He was arrested 1909 at Waterbury, Conn., charged with interfering with the law in the case of Guiseppi A——, who was working the "film-plan game" through the state. After 3 weeks detention he was discharged. Became an American citizen in the autumn of 1910.

The fifth child is Vincenzina (III, 9), b. 1891. She is slight, straight, under five feet tall, has grey-brown eyes, brown hair, muddy complexion, low narrow forehead, high cheek bones, narrow face and high occiput; is illiterate and cannot write her name; has an irritable disposition and even when grown up would tear her hair and cry out on slight provocation; uses bad language. When 13, entered Gair's box factory and was discharged for bad language; worked for three months in a private family, gaining some idea of neatness in personal habits and self-control; has since worked in various places. She became engaged, May 1909, to Guiseppa A—— who was arrested in Connecticut 1909, as stated above, and sentenced for two years. In 1910, she made the acquaintance of John M—— and in January 1911 secured a marriage license at the New York City Hall. This she stated she regarded as a legal marriage, and lived with John M. for a month in a furnished room while she continued to work in a factory for $5.50 per week. J. M. then left her and she secured a warrant for his arrest and went to live with his parents, paying them $3.00 per week board from her earnings. May 1, J. M. returned to her and threatened her. In an altercation, May 12, she stabbed him slightly, was arrested, and held for assault, but later discharged; while John was arrested charged with seduction under promise of marriage.

The sixth child is Sabrino (III, 11), b. 1893; plump and short, with dark complexion, black eyes and hair, full face and attractive expression. She reads and writes in Italian; worked in Gair's box factory from her thirteenth year, earning $4.50 to $7.00 per week. In 1908, she became engaged to Camillo M. (III, 12) eloped with him in the summer of 1909 and married him shortly after. C. M. is tall, brown-haired, illiterate, quick and attractive in manner but indisposed to steady work. In March, 1910, Sabrino became a mother; but her child died a month later and she underwent an operation in the Brooklyn Hospital and remained there until July. She has since worked in the factory at $7.00 per week, but, owing to poor health that requires a doctor's care, she employs herself at home making ostrich feather plumes, at which she earns about $8.00, while her husband, who works on the railroad, sends her monthly or semi-monthly remittances.

The seventh child is Vincenzo (III, 13), b. 1894. He has abundant brown hair and chestnut eyes, ruddy complexion and low forehead. Grew rapidly, and at fifteen, reached five feet ten. Easy-going, companionable, strong, moderately honest and of cheerful disposition; he gambles inordinately and saves nothing; attended public schools irregularly three or four years, but cannot read or write. Found employment without working papers, 1900, calling himself then sixteen, at the Matchless Mfg. Co., 1910, for four months and gave satisfaction. January, 1911, handles newspapers and works thereafter irregularly.

The eighth child is Therese (III, 14), b. 1890 and died 1898.

The ninth child is Mary (III, 15), b. 1899, slight build, brown hair and eyes, fair complexion and a narrow face; she has a good disposition and is always ready to help but is slightly incapable in performance; is slow at school but is passing through the primer. At her mother's death she was sent to St. Joseph's Orphan Asylum, but at Christmas time was taken out by Alfonse A—— to live with a sister, since which time she has attended school irregularly. She learns little at housework, but runs errands.

VI. RECORDS OF NEGRO-WHITE CROSSES.

It is desirable, from many points of view, to *study* the question of the result of negro-white crosses—a question over which so much heat has been raised. Modern studies in heredity justify the conclusion that, under certain circumstances, negro-white crosses might yield, in the second and third generation, *some* persons who had admirable combination of traits, fit to take their place with the best of Caucasian descent.

To test the conclusion, studies have been instituted at the Eugenics Record Office on the method of inheritance of skin color and some other facial traits. The skin color was measured by the color top (color mixer, made by the Milton Bradley Co., Springfield, Mass.), by which means the proportion of black (N), red (R), yellow (Y), and white (W) is quantitatively expressed. The sample selected is that of a Jamaican family: The two grandparents (Gen. I) of whom something is known are mulattoes or approximately so. In the second generation we have children in whose skin color the percentage of black varies from 10 (practically white) to 47. And in the third generation (descended from II, 2 and II, 1) it varies from N 15 to N 40. Thus, some of the children and grandchildren have practically white skins.

A FAMILY HISTORY OF NEGRO-WHITE CROSSES FROM JAMAICA (Fig. 9).

BY FLORENCE H. DANIELSON.

Both Parents of Mixed Blood; the Fraternity Variable in Color.

I. 1. R. B., son of a mulatto woman and the son of a white man and Madagascar woman; brown eyes, black (almost straight) hair, skin color: N 15, R 41, Y 20, W 24.

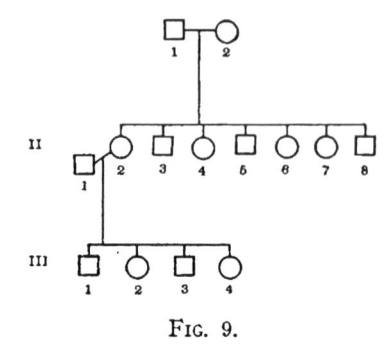

FIG. 9.

I. 2. D. D., daughter of two mulatto parents; hazel or grayish eyes, hair very curly and dark brown, skin color: N 20, R 45, Y 16, W 19. She and I, 1 have nine lawful children of whom 7 are described below (II, 2, 3, 4, 5, 6, 7, 8).

II. 2. R. B., hazel eyes, dark brown somewhat curly hair, skin color: N 11, R 51, Y 20, W 18. Married.

II. 1. R. E., son of black woman and a quadroon man. Brown eyes and nearly typical negro hair, N 25, R 37, Y 20, W 18. They have four children: III, 1, 2, 3, 4.

III. 1. G. E., 10 years; dark brown eyes; curly, decidedly negroid hair; skin color: N 40, R 40, Y 10, W 10.

III. 2. C. E., 8 years, light brown eyes, medium brown curly or wavy hair, skin color: N 35, R 36, Y 15, W 14.

III. 3. L. E., 4½ years, light brown or hazel eyes, medium brown curly or wavy hair, skin color: N 15, R 51, Y 18, W 16.

III. 4. L. E., 2 years, dark brown eyes like father; light brown wavy hair, skin color like III, 3.

II. 3. H. B., at Colon, 30 years, dentist, as dark as II, 8.

II. 4. M. B., at Colon, 26 years; not quite as dark as II, 8, but the darkest of the girls.

II. 5. R. B., 24 years, light brown or hazel eyes, dark brown very curly hair, skin color: N 17, R 44, Y 15, W 24.

II. 6. B. B., 22 years, medium brown eyes, very curly medium brown hair, skin a little tanned: N 20, R 45, Y 18, W 17.

II. 7. M. B., 20 years; gray eyes; dark brown hair, very curly; fairest in family, skin color: N 10, R 49, Y 16, W 25.

II. 8. L. B., 17 years, light brown eyes, almost typical hair; darkest in family, skin: N 47, R 41, Y 16, W 16.

VII. RECORDS OF THE FEEBLE-MINDED AND PAUPERS.

a. THE FIELD WORKER'S REPORT.

An important part of the investigations of our field workers has been tracing the family history of the feeble-minded, including paupers. To the inquiry, who are the feeble-minded? the only answer that can be given is that they are the socially inadequate; who lack one or more traits that are necessary for them to take their part in forwarding the world's work under the conditions of competition afforded by the society in which they live. If they fail in their part they become private or public charges or a social menace.

One history of a family of the feeble-minded from a rural community, is given, with its chart (Fig. 10), below.

FAMILY HISTORY OF EMMA H.

BY H. T. REEVES.

I. 1. William H, *feebleminded* (moron) lived in a little log cabin on the farm belonging to the father of Mrs. Fannie L an old lady living in —— —— Co., N. J. He was sick for a long time before he died and was "on the town."

I. 2. Annie A, wife of William, no data obtainable at present. Children of William H and Annie A were:

II. 1. John H who never married; died of small pox.

II. 2. Peter H, *feebleminded,* who married Sarah H. III, 9. There were no children by this marriage.

II. 3. George, was not bright, stuttered. Married Mary D.

II. 4. Susan H, *feebleminded,* married Joseph H who met his death accidentally by drowning. Nothing can be learned of the cause of Susan's death.

II. 5. William H, *feebleminded,* born March 12, 1819, died May 8, 1869, of tuberculosis.

11. 6. Jane B, born July 23, 1822, came of low grade family, living in the mountains near F——. The family seems to have disappeared. Jane was insane; the trouble seems to have been acute mania according to description. She would have periodic spells of raving and finally drowned herself. The date of her death is not given in the family Bible and no one whom I interviewed could enlighten me.

II. 7. Sarah B, died Jan. 31, 1850.

II. 8. Lydia B, died March 4, 1848.

III. 4. David H, first child of William H and Jane B, born January 27, 1843. This old man is decidedly *feebleminded* and has been "on the town" once or twice, at present he is living with George B at —— ——, N. J., and is able to do enough work about the farm to pay for his board and clothes. David's first wife, Euphemia H has been dead about 30 years. He married his second wife, Anna Jane B, Jan. 14, 1909. This woman is very defective, was the widow of a man by the name of W——, by whom she had three children: Jennie, born

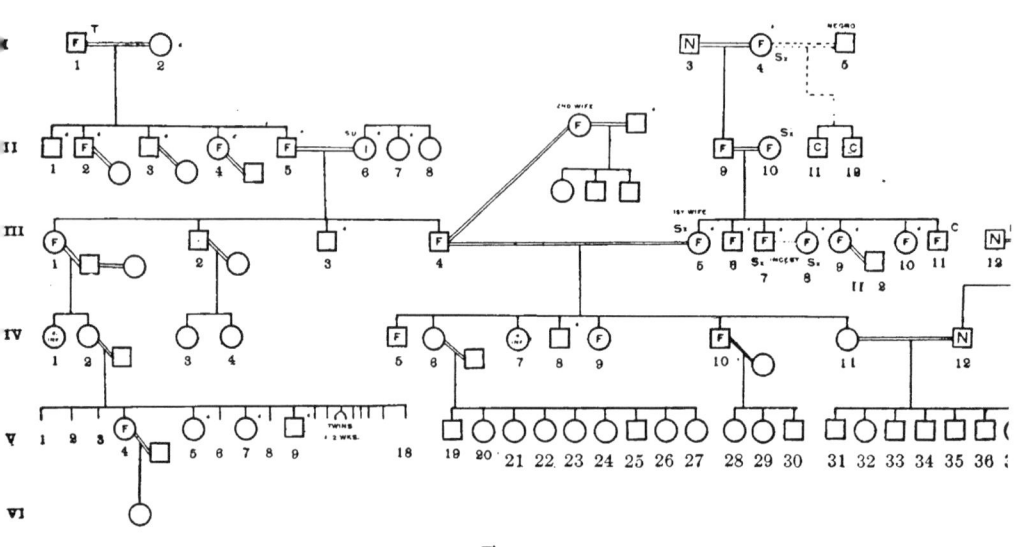

FIG. 10.

September 9, 1887; Joseph, born Jan. 7, 1890; and Robert W——, born August 29, 1893.

David had three brothers and sisters: III, 1, Catherine Ann, *feebleminded,* who married William W of C. She had two children, one died in infancy of measles, the mother dying at nearly the same time from this disease. The other child, Mary Ann, born Oct. 21, 1869 was a very tiny infant when her mother died, but lived to grow up. She married a laborer by the name of James H and has had eighteen children, of whom 13 have lived so far. Mary Ann's step-mother declared all the children were bright with the exception of Nellie F, V 4, who went to school for thirteen years and could never learn to read or write. Nellie is married to a man by the name of H and is living out in the country somewhere. I tried to find the H family—they are living in P——, but as yet have not located them.

III. 2. Is John H, born April 18, 1853, the youngest of this family. His mentality is better by far than that of his brother, David. He and his family live at A——. Interviewed them at suppertime. They did not seem to be at all perturbed by my apparently inopportune visit. John does not appear to be feebleminded. So far all information I have been able to get concerning him has been to the effect that he is "all right." His two daughters are bright girls, both of them are working at present in a shirt factory in the neighborhood. The opinions concerning John's wife all agree that "she isn't what she ought to be, and leads a bad life most of the time." She is a large, fine-looking woman, with a hard-featured and decidedly sensual face. She often has deserted John and lived for varying lengths of time with other men, but John has always taken her back when she has returned from these expeditions, thereby showing much patience or much indifference —it is difficult to tell which.

III. 3. Is George H, born December 21, 1846. He died when he was a small boy.

As has been stated, David III, 4 married Euphemia H who comes of low stock. Mrs. L of N—— G—— told me much concerning her pedigree: The earliest known ancestor was Henry H, who came of good family. The H——'s of the present day are normal, well-respected persons of affairs in the community. Henry married Old Sal I, 4 who came of a tribe of mountaineers called B. Whether this was a surname or nickname the old people of N—— G—— would not tell me. After Henry's death, Old Sal who was *feebleminded* lived with a negro by the name of P. By him she had two halfbreed sons, Coon II, 11 and Jack II, 12. These two boys were the terror of the neighborhood on account of their *criminalistic* tendencies, and both served terms in state's prison. H H and S B had one son who was deficient, Peter II,9. He married Kate G, who was also *feebleminded* and a sex pervert as well. Their children were of varying degrees of deficiency as follows:

III. 6. William Henry, *feebleminded,* very little is known of this man as he died years ago. It is supposed that he never married.

III. 7. Elisha, *very deficient* indeed; he never married but was the father of a child born to his sister Kate Ann, III, 8, who was also of extremely low mental grade. It is just possible that the existence of this child may be traced. It was born in the H—— county poorhouse about thirty years ago.

III. 9. Sarah who married Peter H.

III. 10. Susan, feebleminded, who never married.

III. 11. Jesse who was "lacking" but who had sense enough to steal his sister Euphemia's savings and decamp. He is supposed to be still living somewhere in the middle West.

III. 5. Euphemia was next to the youngest. She was not very feebleminded, but was decidedly a "little off." She never could learn to count, even though Mrs. L's children tried hard to teach her. She was in the home of Mrs. L for about seven years and married David H, August 30, 1868. Her first child IV, 5 William is *feebleminded,* and has the reputation of being the village fool. (b. Oct. 9, 1869.)

IV. 6. Charles E, born Nov. 26, 1871. This man is said to be "all right" by those who have known him all his life. He is a pleasant looking man, vigorous and does not show any stigmata of any sort. He is extremely shiftless and lazy, however, is a tenant farmer but all the buildings and implements about the little farm he has rented showed neglect. There is nothing about his appearance that reminds one at all of his father, "Old Dave"; it is quite possible considering the loose morals of his mother who "went after the men" that his parentage is not what it is supposed to be. At all events he is a borderline case undoubtedly, as is also his wife, Rose C, a cheerful, loquacious person who was ready to show off her brood of nine dirty, noisy, ill-kept children. The oldest child is 12 years old. It will take some time before their mentality can be determnied, but I learned their names and ages.

V. 19. George, was away at work; b. 1899.

V. 20. Stella, also away at work, b. 1900.

V. 21. Mildred, b. 1903.

V. 22. Florence, b. 1904.

V. 23. Irene, b. 1906.

V. 24. Rilly, Irene's twin sister.

V. 25. John, b. 1907.
V. 26. Wilhelmina, b. 1909.
V. 27. Ruth, b. 1910.

Going back to the fourth generation, IV, 7 is Jane, who died at the age of two years, and IV, 8 is Alva L, who died in infancy. IV, 9 is Emma who is at the State Institution in Vineland. She was born Dec. 18, 1879. Has proved to be a trainable case. Helps in the dining room, is a member of the gymnasium class, etc.

IV. 10. Is Ben, who has not yet been interviewed. He was born Oct. 2, 1881, and has so many pecularities of temper he may be justly classed with his feebleminded brothers and sisters. He is of a *wandering* disposition and finds it hard to stick to one job for any length of time. In 1906 he married Minnie B and is living with his three small children somewhere near C.

Annie, the youngest child of David and Euphemia was born March 15, 1886. She is another borderline case; is quite pretty and shows no noticeable defect though she is reported to be rather "soft and silly and not very bright." She married Charles H, a normal man and has seven children who offered a pleasing contrast to those of Elwood and Rose, even though they were almost as dirty and neglected looking.

V. 31. John Sharp M H, b. June 14, 1901.
V. 32. Marion M, b. June 8, 1902.
V. 33. Charles, b. Oct. 30, 1903.
V. 34. Raymond, b. Nov. 8, 1905.
V. 35. Walter, b. Feb. 3, 1907.
V. 36. Roy, b. April 19, 1908.
V. 37. Elizabeth, b. Feb. 23, 1911.

Charles H, IV, 12, comes of good parentage, his father is William H who has been blind for fifteen years, his mother IV, 13 was Mary B who is perfectly normal as far as the character of feeblemindedness is concerned and comes of normal stock.

IV. 12. William H, is related distantly.

b. Description of a Family of the Feeble-Minded.

A fragment to illustrate the style of description suitable for publication.

This fragment is of the Nam family, of which over 800 persons are known, and have been analyzed (Fig. 10).

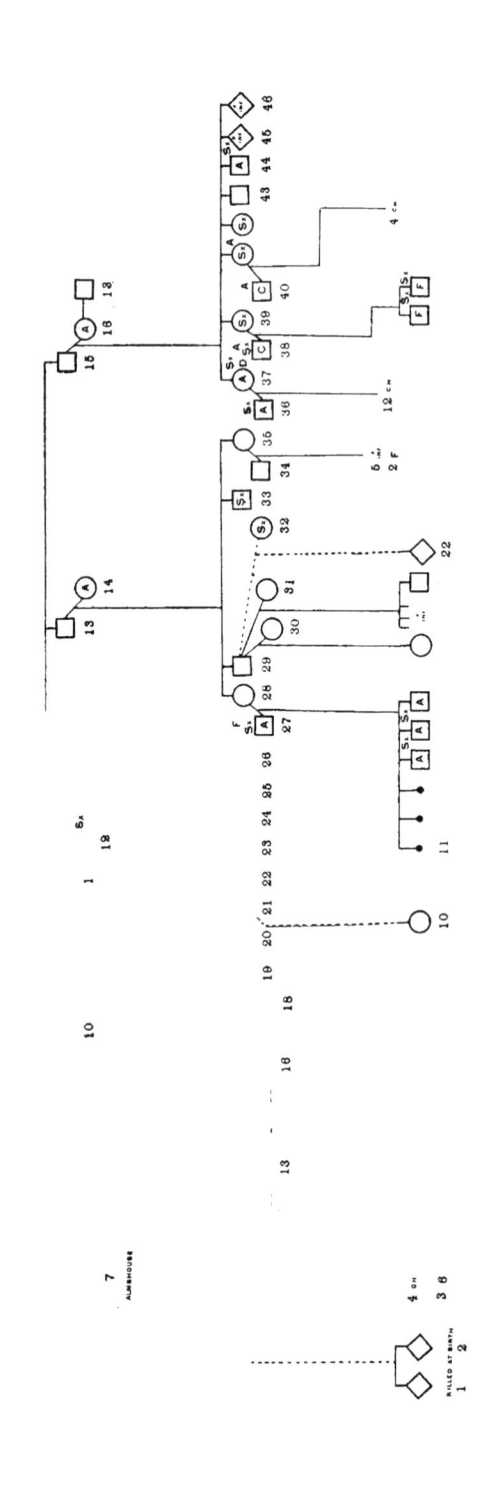

THE NAM FAMILY.

(Compiled from Data Gathered by Dr. A. H. Estabrook.)

From I, 1 were derived two sons and a daughter (II, 1, 3, 4). One son (II, 1), an incapable pauper, broke into a store in F——, for which he served a term in state's prison. The other son (II, 3) was an indigent woodsman. The daughter (II, 4) was chaste, self-esteeming, civil and neat; she died in 1865 of old age.

II, 1 married an unambitious, alcoholic and doubtless deficient woman and had by her three children. Of these, III, 1, was lazy and alcoholic. He got a pension as an ex-soldier in the Civil War, and was a pauper receiving out-door aid; died of cerebral hemorrhages. He married III, 2, licentious in youth and alcoholic, who bore him eight children (IV, 2, 3, 6, 8, 10, 11, 13, 15) all of Nam Hollow. The first, IV, 2, was a suspicious, causationless, alcoholic harlot who married a cousin (IV, 1), a slow, unambitious, honest, chaste, illiterate man, equipped with a good memory but of no initiative or reasoning power; a pauper living in a shack in Nam Hollow; a man derived from an honest father but slattern mother, and of low stock. She, IV, 2, died in 1907 of pleuropneumonia. The progeny, which will be described under Line E were all typical Nams, indolent and unable to learn at school, the men alcoholic and the women harlots.

The next, IV, 3, was an indolent, inefficient, alcoholic, illiterate man, who lived in N. H. successively with 2 women; had three children, and died in 1903 of dropsy. He had by IV, 4, a harlot who died of tuberculosis in 1893, two children, V, 1, of whom the latter died young. Their mother's fraternity, of Canadian origin, was not without mechanical ability, but full of licentiousness. The son, V, 1, though licentious, showed the influence of the outside blood in his ambition, temperance, and pride in his personal appearance. The other woman, IV, 5, was a cousin, incapable of learning, indolent, alcoholic, and a harlot. She was in the House of Refuge for Women, where her child was born, in a number of other correctional institutions, in various houses of prostitution; cohabited with an Italian in New York, where she contracted syphilis, and died in 1908 of pulmonary tuberculosis. This belongs to one of the worst strains of the Nams, which we shall consider later. The ten-year old son of this pair, V, 47, is a stubborn, uncontrollable mischief-maker who ran away from the orphan asylum where he had been placed. The next member of the Nam fraternity, IV, 6, is active, industrious, ingenious, somewhat ambitious but an alcoholic man who married his cousin, IV, 7, a woman whose sense of causation is absent, has hysteria, is called "crazy," and has received temporary aid during four years, and has lived in the county house almost continuously from 1894 to 1902. Died, 1905, of pleurisy. Her fraternity shows typical Nam laziness, together with much taciturnity. From this pair came six offspring, of which two died soon after birth. The eldest son, V, 4, was lazy and unambitious, disorderly when intoxicated, and has cohabited with his equally disorderly and alcoholic sister and has had by her two children, who were both destroyed by the mother at birth. There remains a Nam-like, alcoholic son, V, 6, who works rather steadily at wood-chopping. He has cohabited for the past seven years with his cousin, V, 7, an active, talkative but mentally retarded girl, with complex sex relations. Of their four children, all born in Nam Hollow, one died at six months, the others (6 to 3 years old) are shy and slow. We come now to:

IV, 8 with the slow, unambitious, quiet traits of most Nams. Though alcoholic, he is a good worker and with the help of his son, IV, 19, has recently completed a new house. He married a cousin. IV, 9, (sister of 7, described a few lines above; slow, listless, shy, taciturn, unambitious, illiterate, eccentric, like her sister at times) and had by her nine children of whom 5 died young. The first, V, 14, b. 1879, has some of the best traits of this line; active, industrious, neat, orderly, she has the impulse to do well and lives in much better circumstances than others in the Hollow. By V, 13, an indolent, unambitious, alcoholic, licentious man who later deserted her, and served a prison term for non-support, she had three children, of whom one girl has the mental and moral traits of her mother; the other girl at 13 is feebleminded, licentious and intemperate, while the 8 year old boy is lagging, careless and always in mischief, and runs away from home. The second of the fraternity (V, 15, b. 1885) is indolent and unambitious, did poorly at school is mildly intemperate and licentious at times. Married a cousin. The next, V, 17, b. 1887, is a Nam-like alcoholic, licentious male; a stammerer and a fitful worker; he recently married a feebleminded cousin. Finally, V, 19 is an active, industrious, thrifty, temperate and somewhat chaste young man who owns a pair of horses and helped his father build a house.

To go back a generation, we come next to IV, 10, b. 1860, lazy, died of tuberculosis, 1880. Then comes IV, 11, a Nam-like male, alcoholic and formerly licentious, married to a cousin IV, 12, who is active, industrious, unambitious and irascible, does house **work and** earns all that is brought into the family; a harlot and alcoholic. Lives m poverty in a hovel near A———. Of nine children, seven (V, 20-26) survive. We have now by inbreeding defectives reached nearly a pure type. The six sons are practically all alike in showing the typical Nam traits, including alcoholism and (with possibly two exceptions) licentiousness. The only daughter, b. 1887, is feebleminded, has committed incest with her brothers, and has an illegitimate daughter, 5 years old, slow and bashful. Next comes IV, 13, b. 1850, an industrious, ingenious man of irascible temper and considerable mechanical ability, though with little ambition. Always poor, he had 8 children by three women, and died in 1901 of pneumonia. He first married his cousin, IV, 14, an indolent, indigent harlot, who died 1887, of uterine hemorrhage. She belongs to a large fraternity of Line E, of whom the majority are slow, unindustrious and licentious, although there are striking exceptions. Of their four children the first is slow, deficient in causation, illiterate; lives in poverty and squalor, taking in washing for a living. She married, but soon left him to marry her cousin, V, 27, a feebleminded, licentious drunkard, of a licentious strain. She has 3 miscarriages and three sons (b. 1885 and 1890) all unambitious, alcoholic and licentious, and all living in poverty at I. The next child is V, 29. He gets industry, ingenuousness and mechanical ability from his father's side (or both sides) of the house. His marital relations are complicated. He married his cousin, V, 30, (as described) to legitimatize her feebleminded daughter; then left her and married V, 31 by whom he had 4 children (VI, 18-21); then abandoned her, went to the western part of the state and there cohabited with his stepmother, V, 32 and had an illegitimate child by her in 1911. His principal wife, (V, 31), was active, busy, orderly, neat, good-natured, neither loquacious nor taciturn, but a harlot. Besides V, 29, she has lived with VI, 303, and has had an illegitimate child besides; is now tubercular; lives in New York. Of their four children, 3 died in infancy of alimentary diseases. The 13 year old son is doing fair work in school, is taciturn and unambitious. His sex instincts have not yet broken into flame. V, 33 has also mechanical ability but lack of training. He is quiet, shy, taciturn and licentious; works on a farm in B———. V, 35 is industrious and fairly capable in housework. Married at 16 and had 8 children, of whom 5 died in infancy and two are feebleminded; the other is an infant.

Finally, IV, 15, is a steady but unambitious worker, a Civil War veteran, who was always poor, married a cousin, IV, 16, and died 1881, of cancer of the stomach. She was slow, careless, indifferent, submissive, causationless, unambitious, without initiative, and alcoholic. She had 8 children (VI, 133-40) by IV, 15, and one by IV, 13, which latter was Nam-like, alcoholic and licentious. IV, 16 is still living in Nam Hollow on a widow's pension of $12 monthly, town aid, and basketmaking. Of the children, V, 45 died at 2 days and V, 46 at 3 weeks. V, 37, b. 1870, N. H., is slow, lazy, disorderly, alcoholic, entirely lacking in causation, licentious in youth, deaf. Does washing and basketmaking, and lives in squalor in a hovel. She married V, 36, a quick, industrious, dishonest, untruthful, alcoholic and licentious man who is careful in his work, but careless in other things. His fraternity carries a history of licentiousness. One of them, IV, 4, we have already become acquainted with as the consort of IV, 3. Of their 12 children, three died early (still-born), two are still young. Of the remaining seven, two boys are capable of learning and are, so far, chaste; two boys are Nam-like, alcoholic, licentious, feebleminded and one of them married his cousin in 1911; one boy of 10 years is an apathetic idiot, can neither talk nor walk, being ataxic. He has had several epileptic seizures since he was one year old, and needs institution care. The elder girl is a feebleminded Nam, has had an illegitimate child, and has since married the father. The younger girl, b. 1888 in N. H., is of special interest, for, when young, she was adopted and reared by a good family in B. She could not advance at school, and is lazy and shiftless, though chaste. When away in Vermont where she now lives, married though childless, she dresses neatly; but when in N. H. she reverts to old slack and slovenly ways; such is the influence of an improved environment.

VIII. RECORDS OF EPILEPSY.

The studies that have been made upon epilepsy indicate that there is usually, if not always, an hereditary weakness or tendency to the disease. The symptoms consist of a disturbance of movements and unconsciousness, of which the commonest forms are violent or slight loss of coordination in either general movements or special muscles. In psychic epilepsy there is merely a loss of consciousness usually lasting a few seconds.

The conditions besides convulsions and loss of consciousness which should be carefully noted are: insanity, in different forms, migraine, hysteria, chorea, fainting spells, alcoholism, syphilis and tuberculosis.

In inquiring as to inciting causes or incidental phenomena, ask about maturity at birth and the nature of the mother's labor; spasms in infancy; teething; injuries to head or spine; and about acute infectious fevers of childhood.

STUDY OF AN EPILEPTIC FAMILY (Fig. 12).

In a little wooden shack, on a mountain side in Northern New Jersey, with little furniture and that of the poorest sort, lived, some

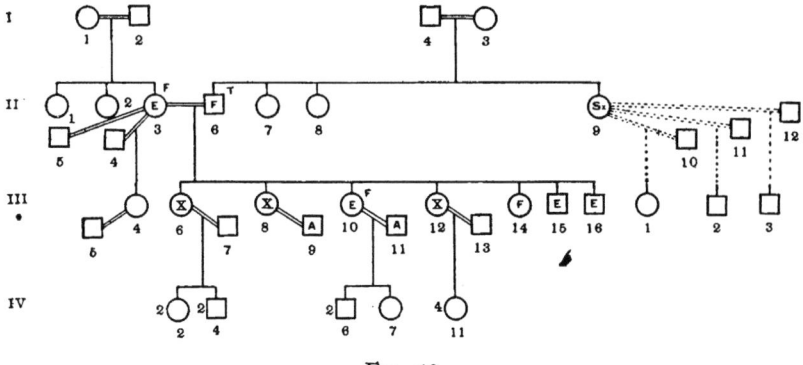

FIG. 12.

years ago, a man and his wife. The man, II, 6, who belonged to old Jersey stock, was shiftless and not infrequently lived for a time in the poorhouse. He was, moreover, a laudanum fiend and is said to have consumed it in large quantities; and he finally died of tuberculosis. One of his sisters, II, 9, was a harlot and had at least three illegitimate children who grew up. Nothing is known about his parents except that his father is said to have been "queer." His wife (II, 3), who still survives, is one of three children, of whom one died in youth, and the other is unknown. She, herself, is without industry or orderliness; clearly mentally defective. She is also an epileptic and has fainting spells which she feels coming on, then screams and faints away. This couple had seven children; concerning three there is little definite information. Of the four others the eldest, a girl, (III, 10, b. 1876), is feebleminded and epileptic. She married a lazy, shiftless alcoholic fellow, III, 11, who has deserted his wife and three young children. The next girl, (III, 14, b. at L. 1870), about whom something is known is likewise feebleminded and, after living for a time in the poorhouse was "placed out," but where she is not even her mother knows. At least one of those with whom she was placed sent her back to the poorhouse. The elder boy, (III, 15, b. at V, 1892), had convulsions shortly before the age of puberty; was "placed out" for a time and has now found his way to a School for Feebleminded Children. The younger boy, b. 1894, began to have convulsions when six years old and he has now found his proper place at the Skillman Village for Epileptics.

IX. RECORDS OF THE INSANE.

Hospitals for the Insane are aware that their Family Histories are quite inadequate—or even false. Careful inquiries made of the families at home reveal an unexpected abundance of mental weakness and aberration.

The following "Guide to Analysis of Personality" has been drawn up by Dr. Amsden and by Dr. August Hoch, Director of the State Psychiatric Institute at Ward's Island, N. Y. It will be found useful by the field worker in pursuit of her investigations.

a. GUIDE TO ANALYSIS OF PERSONALITY:
DRS. GEO. S. AMSDEN AND AUGUST HOCH.

(1) INTELLECTUAL ABILITY
  Ability to learn; how hard did patient have to work in school? Teachers' statements and school reports.
  How capable in positions
  Memory
  Fund of information
  Power of concentration
  Power of observation

(2) OUTPUT OF ENERGY IN WORK AND PLAY
  Lively, active, pushing
  Sluggish, inactive, lazy
  Talkative
  Quiet

(3) HABITS OF ACTIVITY
  Systematic, orderly, punctual, definiteness of purpose
  Desultory
  Demand for precision, consistency
  Efficiency—how responsibility is carried
  Practical or not

(4) MORAL STANDARDS
    Truthfulness, honesty, conscientiousness, or tendency to shirk

(5) GENERAL CAST OF MOOD
    Stable, variable
    Superficial, deep
    Cheerful, optimistic, sense of humor
    Depressive, despondent, anxious, crying easily; moody, with samples of what kind of things caused worry.
    Irritable temper
    Indifferent, placid, phlegmatic

(6) ATTITUDE TOWARDS SELF
    Conceit
    Ability, or inability to see mistakes
    Feeling different from others
    Self-depreciation
    Self-consciousness
    Scruples

(7) ATTITUDE TOWARDS OTHERS
    Sympathetic, kindhearted, affectionate
    Generous
    Selfish
    How does he feel the world treats him?
    Suspicious
    Jealous
    Sensitive—what about?
    Resentful, forgiving   —Topics
    Irritability, temper   —Topics
    Forward
    Bashful
    What did other children think of him?
    Liked or disliked by others

(8) REACTION TO ATTITUDE TOWARDS SELF AND OTHERS
    Frankness   —Does informant know patient's inner life?
    Demonstrative
    Tendency to unburden
    Reticence
    Tendency to seclusiveness
    Brooding   —Topics

Fault finding
Reaction to sensitiveness, jealousy and suspiciousness
Demand for sympathy
How are disappointments taken?

(9) SELF ASSERTION

How much effort does the patient habitually make to shape things or does he allow himself to be carried along?
Independent or dependent on opinion of others
Leader or led
How manage difficulties?
Ambitious
Plucky

(10) ADAPTABILITY

How obedient?
Ability to get along with other children (natural play), or with people in older years
Sociable
Did patient make friends, get readily acquainted?
Ability to take advice
Stubborn
Opinionated

(11) POSITION TOWARDS REALITY

Did patient take things as they are?
Phantastic
Day dreaming

(12) SEXUAL SPHERE

How much occupied with question
In awe of it, or afraid of it, or how was patient's attitude towards it?
Frank or especially secretive about it
Bashful in presence of other sex, or forward
Longings
Reaction to sexual desires
Prudishness

(13) BALANCING FACTORS

Religion, interests
How much satisfaction does patient get from what he does?
Ideals

TABLE OF FORMS OF INSANITY.

(The following terms should not be used to replace description.)

I Organic

        (Accompanying syphilis)
1. General paralysis—paresis
2. Brain syphilis

        (Accompanying alcohol)
3. Delirium tremens
4. Alcoholic dementia—chronic alcoholic psychoses

        (Accompanying arterio-sclerosis)
5. Arteriosclerotic insanity
6. Dementia paralytica

        (Accompanying the general deterioration of old age)
7. Senile dementia

II Functional
1. Manic-depressive insanity
   - hypermania
   - recurrent mania
   - melancholia
   - involutional psychoses
   - puerperal psychoses
2. Dementia praecox
3. Paranoid states (usually combined with 1 or 2)

Equivalents: Disturbed emotional states; e. g. excessive anger, fear, secretiveness, suspicion, jealousy, piety, hilarity, general irritability, obstinacy, cruelty, egotism.

Periodic mental disturbances: sick headaches (migraine), fugue, dipsomania (sprees).

Note if states are recurrent or progressive.

b. RECORD OF THE C—— FAMILY, WITH MUCH INSANITY (Fig. 13).

BY RUTH S MOXCEY.

I. 1. James D. C——, born in M——, Oct. 10, 1804, died of insanity, Apr. 20, 1864. He was a conscientious man, inclined to be hyper-religious, but not so severely as to let religion interfere with

FIG. 13.

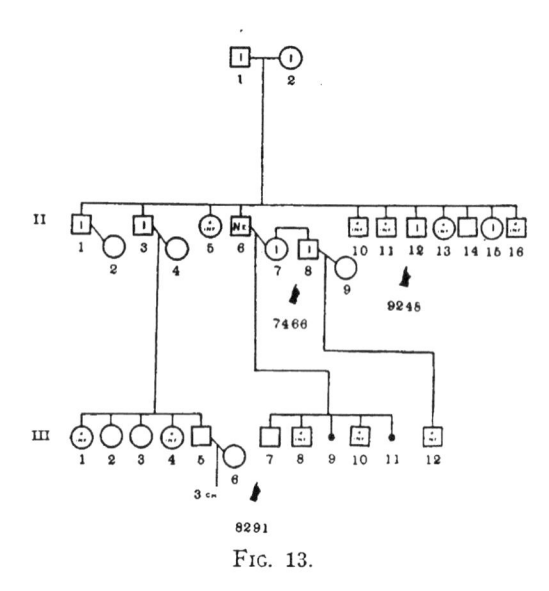

his activity and daily work. On Sundays his religious demonstration was so violent that the young people of M—— were said frequently to attend church from curiosity to see what he would do. "One time he burst the pew door open and sprang suddenly into the aisle; he was always making himself noticeable for the way in which he 'got religion.'" He was also a week-day curiosity, though no one has said why. By telling of some "graft" connected with the M—— poor-farm that had come to his knowledge, he incurred the anger of an overseer who was probably reaping some benefit from the graft. When the latter heard that James had exposed the affair publicly on M—— wharves where he often went fishing, he called at James' house and threatened him for having told. James was much agitated, and worried so much over the matter that he finally went to bed ill. He soon went violently insane, and died in the course of a week.

I. 2. On Nov. 29, 1827, he had married Susan R——, also born in M——. She was also insane upon religion. She had melancholia, and feared that she might not be good enough to go to Heaven when she died; she often cried and moaned over this. Mental trouble came on so gradually that some did not consider it as such until the last four or five years of her life; but all agree that she was unduly concerned about her life, and worried over little or nothing for a period of ten or twelve years before her death, on Jan. 1891 in M——. She had eleven children:

II. 1. James D. C——, b. Feb. 20, 1829, in M——, married Hannah T——, also of M——. There were no children. The wife is still living, but as she has had several paralytic shocks, she is unable to give any information. James D. is said to be a very rigid old-fashioned Baptist. Relatives say that he was subject to religious melancholia, similar to, tho less intense than, that of his mother. He was a shoemaker, but he sat and dreamed over his work. "He held a shoe in one hand, and in the other he held a Bible instead of the necessary hammer." He was never an active man, but was not as "gone on religion" as was his father. He died in Salem Hospital Apr. 27, 1904, of exhaustation—fracture of the thigh, said by relatives to have been caused by a fall when getting out of bed.

II. 3. John C——, b. Dec. 2, 1830, and d. May 10, 1893, of pneumonia and diarrhoea, at C——, Mass., where he had been a nurse in the Soldiers' Home. He had been temporarily insane at various times from the age of 50 and possibly earlier. Many never knew much of this trouble, for J. C. seemed to know when it was coming on, and just what to do for himself when in this condition. A change of place or occupation seemed to help him, and he took care to keep his hands and mind occupied as fully as possible. He also suffered from melancholia.

II. 4. Elizabeth D——, his wife, d. age 53-4, of pulmonary tuberculosis. They had five children:

III. 1. Lizzie, d. inf.

III. 2. Emily, d. Tb., May 18, 1786, age 18-10-13.*

III. 3. Etta (Marietta), unmar., d. April 14, 1889, age 29-7-14, of phthisis.

III. 4. Annie, d. inf.

III. 5. Leonard, married a Swedish woman, lives M——, has 3 children.

II. 5. Susan C——, b. 1832, d. 1839.

II. 6. Thomas R. C—— (father of No. 8291, and bro. of No. 9242) b. Aug. 23, 1834, in M——, d. Dec. 21, 1904, of pleurisy. Shoemaker by trade. His wife says that he was a nervous man, always very frail. He was taken ill with pleurisy one day and died the next at 4 P. M.

II. 7. Susan C—— his wife, and mother of case No. 8291, is living at No. 4 ——— ———, M———. She is an irritable but kindly

---

* Years—months—days.

woman; noted for her religious fickleness and zeal. She has been Baptist, Mormon, and has been in street parades with a tambourine for the Salvation Army. Her cautiousness is at times absurd. She did not tell the physicians in the hospital of a serious blow her son received on the head from a fall a short time previous to his being sent to the hospital, for fear that they might wish to "have some sort of an operation to see if that was what caused his mental trouble." She is at first suspicious, but can be won to give confidence, tho she worries afterward for fear she has said too much. She has friends whom she trusts implicitly, and her suspicious caution toward others whom she does not favor, seems never to be entertained towards friends. She takes "summer folk" to room with her at the beach, and she has for some years taken "fresh air" children, tho she has not done that recently as she is becoming too elderly to care for them. She has an eccentric habit of leaving her housework and walking the streets or visiting neighbors at meal time and taking the key with her so that her husband upon his return would find the house locked and no meals prepared. She says that her eyes will not allow her to work, but told of reading a novel until midnight. She had 3 children and two miscarriages:

III. 8. (No. 8291) Foster C——, b. Jan. 11, 1869, in M——. Admitted to hospital June 13, 1896, age 27, machinist, unmarried. Primary Dementia. "Confusion, disorientation, auditory hallucinations, hyper-religiosity, mutism, tendon reflex exaggerated, irritability, incoherence, psychomotor excitement, violent acts, motor restlessness, negativisim, masturbation, violent threats, stupor." Physicians certif: "Excited, dangerous, violent. Of late he has become more violent, and has escaped from home several times, causing disturbance in the street. While in bed, used profane language; said he had given up religion and gone to swearing." Note of May 22, 1911: "An exam. of chest at time of transfer to T. B. showed no signs; patient began to gain flesh and eat better immediately upon going out, and has continued to gain up to the present time, weighing now about 140 lb. Mental condition unchanged. Sits about with his head bowed, talking to himself. When questioned, answers in a quick, peculiar voice." He was working on a stationary engine, in connection with the laying of some street sewers in Feb., previous to his confinement in June. His work was in M——. One night he stayed overtime because the man who should have relieved him was intoxicated. He became very weary, and finally when he was relieved, he slipped on an icy side-walk, striking his head so severely that he "saw stars" for some time; he was not certain that he was unconscious at all, and as soon as he got up, he started for his home in M——, some miles distant.

  III. 8. George S—— C——, b. March 28, 1872; and d. July 25, 1872. M—— record gives cause: "Infantile."

  III. 9. Miscarriage, 3 mo. "Went for a carriage ride, and came home sick."

  III. 10. Frederick B—— C——, b. M——, Jan. 28, 1876; d. Feb. 4, 1877, of diphtheria.

  III. 11. Miscarriage, 2 mo. from cleaning house.

  II. 10. Joseph C——, b. Sept. 28, 1836; d. Sept. 26, 1837.

  II. 11. Joseph C——, b. Oct. 19, 1838; d. Aug. 30, 1839.

  II. 12. (No. 9242) Joseph C——, b. Aug. 8, 1841; admitted to hospital Oct. 19, 1898; shoemaker, unmarried. Diag.: Primary Dementia—Physical deformity (has a shoemaker's deformity of the lower end of the sternum.); dementia, disorientation, hernia, visual hallucinations, heredity, incoherence, mannerisms, sunstroke, suicidal acts, obscenity, motor restlessness, varicose veins, reflex changes, exaggerated. Physician's certificate: "Attempted suicide more than 25 years since. Said he did not feel well; does not drink much water; did not think the water in the well was fit to use in watering plants; sat still and talked; had used obscene and insulting language towards different individuals; wandered about the streets at night. No change in mental and physical condition in past 25 years." Patient is still in this hospital; used to work on the ward, but does nothing now. Talks to himself continually. Knows the name of the President of the U. S. and knows that hospital has a new superintendent this spring.

  II. 13. Susan C——, b. Oct. 8, 1843; d. Nov. 16, 1844.

  II. 14. Samuel R. C——, b. Oct. 8, 1846; d. Sept. 16, 1847.

  II. 15. Mary Susan C—— (now Mrs. Philip C——, No. 33 —— ——, M——). She is decidedly a psychopathic personality. She has mannerisms, is very suspicious, untruthful, and in a minute forgets what she has told so that, by cross-questioning, one can obtain some things from her. As soon as some of her family come into the room she ceases telling what is incorrect, and when she sees that others are willing to talk, she sits as if she had been eager to be of service from the first, and begins to talk incessantly, but cautiously withholding facts. Have often met her in the streets in M——; she walks rapidly with her head down, and a sidewise glance from under her lowered brow is taking in everything, tho she apparently thinks no one knows she is looking. She always endeavors to get past without salutation (and she seems to do this with all she meets on the street); but when spoken to, she looks up and responds in the same words, then hurries on head down. She did not marry until middle age. Her husband, an old soldier, a cripple, cooks in a good "sea-food" restaurant in M——.

II. 16. Edward D. C——, b. Apr. 11, 1840 and d. Sept. 4, 1849.

II. 8. (No. 746) Nicholas F. P——:

Susan C. P——, the mother of the patient (Case No. 8291), has also a brother in hospital (746, 228); age at last admit., 35; age at 2nd admit., 47; Apr. 11, 1882; assigned cause, intemperance, but no diagnosis appears. History at that time by sister: "Patient is of fair mental capacity; no religious belief; common school education; cheerful disposition and industrious habits; shoemaker; for two years has been a hard worker; one uncle died from brain softening; no history of hereditary insanity; is said to have enjoyed good physical health with the exception of partial sunstroke received some years ago. In June, the patient, after a long debauch, became very apprehensive; expressed delusions of persecution; said he heard people about his house, and refused to go out for fear of injury. After a week of absentation from drink, became better and returned to work. Began drinking and soon began to complain of headache and to exhibit delusions of fear. For six weeks has been actively deluded, imagining himself an object of persecution by the liquor sellers of the town. Has refused to go out of the house and has eaten and slept irregularly; no attempt at self-injury has been made. Thinks the rum sellers have put him down as a 'spotter.'" June 14, 1882, discharged as recovered. He was returned in March 22, 1894. Physician's certificate: "He has been insane for 15 years, and has lately become violent at times." Hospital rec.: "Alcohol, apprehensiveness, dementia, allopsychic delusion, exaltation, auditory hallucinations, indifference, incoherence, mannerisms, violent acts." Hospital: "Since note of March 26, 1905, the patient is reported continually as a tidy, useful person, well oriented, contented to stay here." He was married some time between the two commitments; his record says that he had been an inmate of the M—— almshouse for many years. His sister Susan says that one child was b. to him thru his marriage to Adeline S——:

III. 12. George, d. age 6-7 years in L——. The child as described was born with a tumor in his back, one joint of his spine was missing and this bunch was there in place of it.

The sister who gave the history of 2nd admit. said that "Father died of heart disease; mother died of spinal trouble."

c. HUNTINGTON'S CHOREA.

A form of chorea that leads to dementia. This disease well illustrates the method of inheritance of a *dominant* trait, since it never "skips a generation."

RECORD OF A CASE OF HUNTINGTON'S CHOREA (Fig. 14).

BY DR. E. B. MUNCEY.

Elizabeth P. I, 1 (5th generation from S. B. and R. F.) was born 1822 in C——, Onondaga County, N. Y. Married A. K. C., I, 2. They

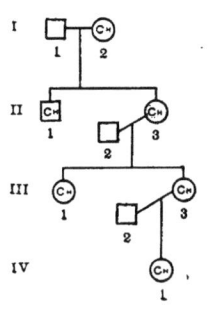

FIG. 14.

lived in V. B. New York for several years and later removed to G. She had chorea badly before death.

They had two children, II, 1, and P. C., II, 2, both suffered with chorea in a pronounced form. The history of Philo, II, 1, is not known.

P. C., II, 2, lived in M. where she married S. W., II, 3. They had two children.

E. W., III, 1, and her father lived in G. where she carried on dressmaking until her choreic movements became so pronounced that she was obliged to give it up. After this she became rapidly worse and died a few years ago (date uncertain) from exhaustation due to constant muscular movements. Her mind was seriously impaired. She died unmarried.

E. W. was affected earlier in life than her sister; onset between 25 and 30 years, soon after the birth of her baby. She married a man named M., and removed from G. Their daughter E. M. was choreic

she is looking. She always endeavors to get past with
(and she seems to do this wh all she meets on the street
spoken to, she looks up and esponds in the same words,
on head down. She did not arry until middle age. Her
old soldier, a cripple. cooks i a good "sea-food" restauran

II. 16. Edward D. C——. b. Apr. 11. 1840 and d. S
II. 8. (No. 746) Nicolas F. P——:

Susan C. P——. the moer of the patient (Case
also a brother in hospital (74 228) : age at last ad: it
admit.. 47; Apr. 11. 1882 assigned cause. inte.
diagnosis appears. History a that time by sister:
mental capacity; no religious belief: common sch
ful disposition and industrios habits; shoemaker;
been a hard worker; one une died from brain so
of hereditary insanity; is sai to have enjoyed g
with the exception of partial sunstroke received s(
June, the patient. after a leg debauch. became vt
expressed delusions of persetion; said he heard
house, and refused to go ot for fear of injury
absentation from drink. becae better and returned
drinking and soon began to plain of headache a
lusions of fear. For six weeks has been actively d
himself an object of persecution by the liquor sei
Has refused to go out of the buse and has eaten an l
no attempt at self-injury has ien made. Thinks the
put him down as a 'spotter.'" June 14, 1882. dischar
He was returned in March 22:894. Physician's certi
been insane for 15 years, an has lately become .
Hospital rec.: "Alcohol, apprehensiveness, dement
lusion, exaltation, auditory hlucinations, indiffer
mannerisms, violent acts." Hspital: "Since r
the patient is reported continuay as a tidy, u
contented to stay here." He as marrie
commitments; his record says at he
almshouse for many years. Is si
b. to him thru his marriage

III. 12. George, d. ag
scribed was born with a tum
missing and this bunch was

his mother,
ells which are

married 8 years,

own.
old. She was born in
in Iowa. Her general
features and a pleasant
and left in the fifth grade,
in part by interruptions.
us trouble. She has always
When 15 years old she had an
re, and, in consequence spent a
h married III, 11, giving her age
wh her husband for two months
s had two spasms since her marriage.
nat he husband sent her away because

or to figure. He works in the
was once shot at. His mother
arried.

from birth. As they left G. when she was a small child further history was unavailable.

X. RECORDS OF THE CRIMINALISTIC.

Studies already made suffice to indicate that in many crimes the act is a result of mental condition which is inherited. This is particularly true of crimes against chasity, drunkenness, incorrigibility, truancy, vagrancy, crimes against the person, arson, larceny, and malicious mischief of the grosser sorts. The study of the family history frequently enables a judgment to be drawn as to the relative importance of a bad environment and a bad nervous constitution in these cases. In criminal trials of the future it is certain that more consideration will be given to hereditary tendencies for whose possession the individual is clearly not responsible.

HISTORY OF A CRIMINALISTIC FAMILY IN NARRATIVE FORM.

DATA FURNISHED BY MRS. MARY DRANGA, KINDNESS OF DR. W. M. HEALY
(Fig. 15).

A robust locomotive fireman now 68 years old who uses no alcohol or tobacco, and of whose antecedents nothing is known, married, many years ago, II, 2, a woman who was born in the mountains of West Virginia, near the Kentucky line. Though illiterate, this woman is physically well developed, fine looking, clean, and a hard worker. She has, however certain clear mental defects. She is subject to headaches on both sides of the head, accompanied with nausea, so that she must sometimes keep to her bed for a week. She has also fainting spells in which she shakes and falls down, sometimes bruising herself. Her eyeballs roll up, she can recall nothing about the spasm after it is over, but gets up, and goes to work, though with a sleepy feeling. She has 2 or 3 of these spells each week and has had them for a long time. She uses tobacco and alcohol in considerable amount and has the reputation of using morphine. Her temper is at times violent and she has been brought to court for abusing her daughter Ella. She steals from houses where she works. Finally, she was a harlot before her marriage while in West Virginia, and since her marriage cannot keep away from men. She has had 10 children by her husband; the biography of some of them has been ascertained.

III. 1. This son killed two men in W. of whom one was a policeman. His sister Ella informed on him, but he got off with slight penalty. Ella has been obliged to avoid her brother since.

III, 4 is the next daughter. She lives in West Virginia, has been married twice and has three children. While living with her second husband she had a paramour. In collusion with her, he shot her husband in the head, killing him, and she now lives with this murderer, whom she freed from the law by false witnesses.

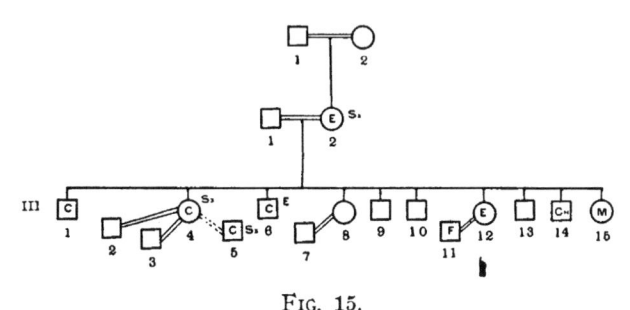

FIG. 15.

III, 6 is a man of 21 years. He is sickly, and, like his mother, an inveterate user of tobacco, and liable to fainting spells which are doubtless epileptic in nature.

III, 8 is a woman of good reputation, has been married 8 years, is childless, lives in Virginia.

III, 9, 10 are two sons of whom nothing is known.

III, 12 is a young woman not quite 17 years old. She was born in West Virginia but since the age of 11 has lived in Iowa. Her general physical condition is good, she has regular features and a pleasant square face. She was at school for 6 years and left in the fifth grade, but her slow progress is to be explained in part by interruptions. There is clear evidence of serious nervous trouble. She has always been nervous and afraid in her sleep. When 15 years old she had an hysterical attack, following a slight scare, and, in consequence spent a month in a hospital. A little later she married III, 11, giving her age as 18 instead of 16. After living with her husband for two months he sent her to Chicago. She has had two spasms since her marriage. Letters from her home stated that her husband sent her away because he found her with a man.

III, 11 is unable to write his name or to figure. He works in the round house of the railroad, where he was once shot at. His mother lives with a man to whom she is not married.

III, 13 is a son, nothing known about him.

III, 14 is a son who died at 13 years. Had St. Vitus' dance and heart trouble.

III, 15, 13 years old. Has bad headaches with nausea, so that she has to go to bed for a day or two.

XI. RECORDS OF SEX OFFENSE.

The problem of prostitution in our cities cannot be solved by visiting brothels and making inquiries of the inmates, on the assumption that they are quite like other people excepting that they are the victims of an unfortunate environment. It is necessary to make a psychological analysis of the prostitute's fraternity and that of her father and mother. It appears at once that her traits were born with her—are in her blood.

The following is a schedule of inquiries that should, at the diseretion of the field worker, be made.

PERSONAL HISTORY
Date of birth
Place of birth
Nature of early surroundings: urban, rural, etc.
Care by mother, by sisters, by brothers, by servants.

ECONOMIC HISTORY

SEXUAL HISTORY
First sex feelings; age, nature
Growth of sex knowledge
Masturbation, if any; history.
Onset of menstruation; age, symptoms
History of relations with men; with conditions leading to them and details that throw light on the psychical condition of each of the pair.

PHYSICAL TRAITS
Present height
Present weight
General facial appearance, as to beauty and intelligence.
Eye color
Hair color
General mental ability — Binet test
Appreciation of cause and effect
Appreciation of consequences of sex act
Foresight
Attitude toward social infamy
Love of amusement and excitement
Vivacity
Love of display
Vanity; desire to be noticed
Curiosity

Appetites for alcohol; for narcoties
Industry or idleness
Modesty—sensitiveness to exposure unclad
Self respect

SEX IMPULSE
Tendency to fall in love
Strength of desire
Indulgence in erotic imagination
Strength of inhibitions
Desire for exclusive and permanent possession

DEGREE OF PLEASURE DERIVED THROUGH SENSE OF:

Touch, particularly of persons.
Taste (Idiosyncrasies of).
Color. Music. Smell (personal odors; perfumes)

APPRECIATION OF IDEAS OF:
Sex-immorality, virtue, purity, chastity
Self control
Public opinion
Truth, honesty, kindness (to children and animals)
Trustworthiness and reliability

LIABILITY TO OTHER ANTI-SOCIAL ACTS

FAMILY HISTORY OF AN INMATE OF A GIRLS' HOME (Fig. 16).

BY WINIFRED HATHAWAY.

The Patient, IV, 1, b. Nov. —, 1893, East Boston, Mass. Parents American, Protestant, early environment unfavorable. Father: feeble-minded, immoral, alcoholic, abusive to the children; mother: young, very immoral, worked part time in a store and left the children alone all day. Home poor and neglected, in a bad section of the city. Patient born at full term when mother was less than 15 years old. From childhood she would do anything to attract attention to herself. For instance, when "Jack the Snipper" was cutting the hair of girls in the streets, the patient caused a sensation by cutting off her own hair. She hid it, invented a thrilling story of her encounter with the vandal, was delighted when brought to court, and confessed only when confronted with hair which had been found. She was fairly good at school, reached the eighth grade, but never cared for study. She was untrustworthy, wilful, quick-tempered, crazy over boys; admits she began to have immoral relations at 9 years of age and cannot recall that she ever had any sense of modesty. When she was about 14 years old, her mother left her husband, took the children with her and moved to a house near the Charleston Navy Yard. The patient visited the yard with a companion and, subsequently, under pretence of going to school or to church, she frequently went to the Yard. She represented herself as an officer's daughter, and seems to have had free access to the place at any hour of the day. The companion spoken of above also introduced her to a house of ill-fame. The patient thus described her Sundays: Directly after breakfast she took her Bible and ostensibly started for Sundayschool. Really

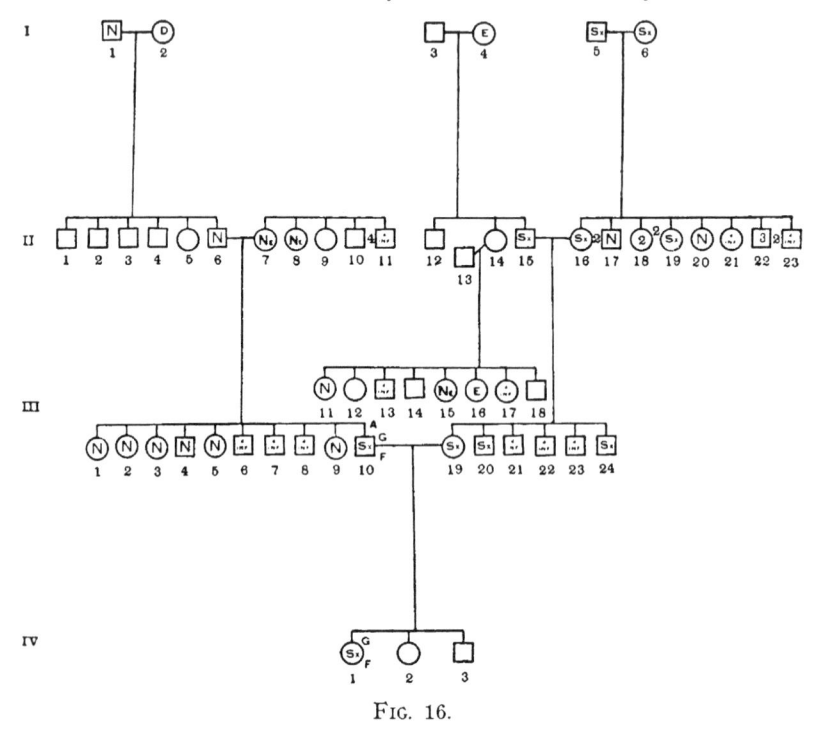

FIG. 16.

she went to the Navy Yard, then returned for dinner, went out again, ostensibly for a walk, but really to a house of ill-fame, remained until late in the afternoon, returned for supper, and sometimes went in the evening to the Navy Yard or to a house of ill fame. Her account of her sexual life may be exaggerated to add to the sensation; but she declares that she had immoral relations with at least 150 marines at the Navy Yard and visited four houses of ill-fame in Boston; she received money but there is no evidence that a desire for it had any important influence in leading her to these places or causing her to continue to frequent them. If left a moment to herself she practices masturbation; she says she cannot keep away from men and that she feels at times that she must go to the Navy Yard.

Her offenses soon became so flagrant that Society began to take notice. In a department store where she worked, she flirted so that three men lost their positions through her and she was discharged. She took a young girl to the Navy Yard where they had immoral relations with marines; the friend was frightened and told someone in authority so that the marines were arrested and sentenced to 2½ years, while the patient herself was put under the care of the Children's Aid Society; was "placed out" by the society into a good family, but her libidinous instincts soon ended this relation. Then her mother had her committed to an institution for wayward girls, 1909, at the age of 16 years. She was placed on parole two years later with a family in D——; here she met two men; was of no use in the household and was returned. Was placed in W—— but was unable to do anything without assistance; placed out in H—— but ran away and was returned to the Institution where she now is.

At present the patient is a goodlooking girl, 5' ¼" tall; weight 122 lbs; has thick, dark wavy hair, (some hairs gray); dark eyes, very full and large and with glasses. Hands thick and voice low and pleasantly modulated. Never noisy, but listless and sentimental with a dreamy superior air very irritating to the other girls. Indolent, always with an excuse to offer against work; smooth, cunning and an inveterate liar. She has gonorrhea and has deteriorated mentally. The Binet test gives 11.4 years. Definitions poor, could not put dissected sentences together, repeat figures or sentences or give rhymes; can do no abstract work or manual work without supervision. She has been diagnosed as deficient in any moral sense, incapable of acquiring it and requiring permanent custodial care.

PATIENT'S FRATERNITY.

Sister, IV, 2, b. 1894, East Boston, Mass. A small, slender girl with brown hair and eyes, rather coarse features, sallow complexion, very bad teeth, forward, incapable, extremely nervous and hysterical. Graduated from the Grammar School and has been attending evening High School this winter. Worked for a time at W's department store, but lost her position for laughing and talking too much; is at present working at H's department store. So far as known she is a moral girl.

Brother, IV, 3, b. 1898, East Boston, Mass. A very small boy for his age; light-brown hair, small blue eyes, small oval face, head rather pointed, ears protruding, has suffered much from abscesses in his neck. Mentality very good. Graduated from the grammar school and is attending the Mechanic's Art School. Does a great deal of the housework, cooks, scrubs, and is altogether very capable. At present is running errands for a dressmaker after school and on Saturdays. He is emotional, cries very easily, is highstrung and nervous.

PATIENT'S FATHER.

III. 10. B. 1868, East Boston, Mass. A slender man of medium height, small head, protruding brown eyes; has a sullen expression; and is sullen and moody in his reactions. It is reported that he had a fall when a child and has been considered half-foolish since. Intoxicants make him almost insane; and, it is said, he has had delirium tremens; he is often called "Crazy C"; and has never amounted to anything. He boarded with a Mrs. A. and there met her daughter, the patient's mother, who was not quite 14; she became pregnant by him, and he was obliged to marry her. He soon began to drink heavily, quarreled with and abused the members of his family, failed to support them, and was several times arrested for non-support; has to pay $4.50 per week toward the support of his children. He was a teamster; helped for a time as school janitor and worked about wharves. Is working at present for a Boston firm.

FATHER'S FRATERNITY.

III. 1. East Boston, a short, very stout woman of excellent repute and average mental ability; married a fireman of good repute. They live in a good, clean tenement in a fair location. Formerly wished to bring up the patient, but her mother refused.

III. 2. B. 1860, East Boston, a short, plump woman of excellent repute and good mentality. Married W. N., a police officer of high rank; live in a clean, comfortable frame house. Have two children, E. N. and E. F. N., of good reputation, the latter of whom is married and has a somewhat backward two year old child.

III. 3. A small woman of good repute and mentality; has two children who are well spoken of.

III. 4. B. 1861, East Boston, a very stout man, brown hair and eyes, features large, nose broad, bridge broken. Is janitor of School ——; has held position 20 years, is considered efficient, and is of good repute.

III. 5. B. ——, of good repute.

III. 6. B. 1863, East Boston, d. 1868, membraneous croup.

III. 7. B. 1865, East Boston, d. 1869, infant wasting.
III. 8. B. 1867, East Boston, d. 1869, infant wasting.
III. 9. B. 1872, East Boston, a short, plump woman, brown eyes, and hair, broad face, small features, bad teeth, mentally good and of good reputation.

PATIENT'S FATHER'S FATHER AND HIS FRATERNITY.

II. 6. B. 1836, East Boston, Mass. A very stout man only 4 feet tall, of excellent repute, a school janitor for 40 years. Suffered from cataracts and bladder trouble, operated at hospital on eyes, and died 1912.

II. 1. B. about 1832, East Boston, was a ship rigger, fell from rigging and was killed 1860.

II. 2. B. 1834, East Boston, of good repute, married, several children, d. 1904 of complication of diseases.

II. 3. B. 1838, East Boston, Mass. A tall, well-built man. Gray hair and beard, blue eyes; keen kindly face; of excellent character, married, five children.

II. 4. B. 1841, East Boston, Mass.; moved to California; when young died by suicide.

II. 5. Girl, unknown.

PATIENT'S FATHER'S FATHER'S FATHER AND MOTHER.

I. 1. B. 1808, Boston, Mass. Was ship rigger by trade, had sent son into rigging when latter fell to his death. Father never recovered from shock. His wife, I, 2, b. 1821, is reported to have been of excellent character, kept her faculties, except hearing, until her death.

PATIENT'S FATHER'S MOTHER AND HER FRATERNITY.

II. 7. B. 1838 Hingham, Mass. A large-framed fleshy woman, hair black, eyes brown, prominent, face and features large, good mentality and reputation; rather hard and bitter.

II. 8. B. 1836, Hingham, Mass. Was of good repute, milliner by trade, suffered a long time from kidney trouble, became quite *childish* before her death.

II. 9. B. about 1840, d. 1882 of cancer in the side.

II. 10. B. about 1842, d. 1886, Bright's disease.

II. 11. Four children, d. in infancy.

PATIENT'S MOTHER.

III. 19. B. 1878, Nova Scotia. A short, plump exceedingly pretty woman, prematurely gray hair, large blue eyes, with a trick of looking very child-like and innocent that is apt to lead one astray. Round face, plump cheeks, good complexion, large nose, full mouth, pleasant voice and manners, average intelligence, a great talker, but wholly superficial. Very emotional and hysterical; rather fond of weeping, a hard-working woman; a sales-woman at a large department store doing house-work, washing, cooking, and sewing evenings and Sundays. Is very neat in her personal appearance, cannot bear to have the children wear store-made things, and the fact that the patient had on prison-made shoes at the Home seemed to hurt her more than all the immorality. The small tenement where she lives is fairly clean, the home always quiet; she represents herself to be a widow. She is reported always to have been a sensual girl, attracted the attention of men wherever she went. Her mother kept a boarding house in East Boston, and the girl was around the boarders a great deal. When she was 13 years old her mother went to Nova Scotia, leaving her at the boarding house. She is reported to have been very intimate with the boarders and when her mother returned she was found to be pregnant. She declared at first that her father was responsible for the child, but admitted that she had relations with III, 10, and asserted that he was the father; finally he married her, before the patient was born. As the children grew up they ran the streets; each parent reproached the other for immorality and though III, 19 pretended to be shocked at the patient's life, it in part reflected her own. Since her separation from her husband, she has received a man by the name of J—— who stays all night. She is said to have bragged about him among the shop girls as her "conquest."

PATIENT'S MOTHER'S FRATERNITY.

III. 20. A very large strong man, who is a teamster. Has been very immoral but seems to have settled down with his wife (A B) whom he was forced to marry. They live with his mother in a good, clean tenement, and have four children.

III. 21, 22. Two boys died at about 2 years of age of diphtheria.

III. 23. Boy, died infancy of cholera infantum.

III. 24. B. 1886, East Boston, Mass. A large, very healthy man, of good mentality, considered the best in the family; but his marriage said to have been a "forced" one. He has two young children.

PATIENT'S MOTHER'S FATHER.

II. 15. B. 1856, Nova Scotia. A very small man, weighing 76 lbs. Has always been very hardworking and much brow-beaten, and never a very successful man. He did night work in a sugar refinery for 30 years, never getting more than $10 a week. He watched the vats and had to keep in a bending position most of the time and to this position and tobacco are ascribed the cancer of the buccal cavity from which he suffers. He had an operation in which the growth was removed but there is no hope of recovery; meanwhile the company continues his salary. It is reported that his wife treated him cruelly, making him do the family washing when he returned from the night's work, striking him on the head and abraiding the skin with a rolling pin, providing him with insufficient food. His marriage was forced for his wife was pregnant by him before her marriage.

HIS FRATERNITY.

II. 12. B. 1850, Nova Scotia, said to be living in Laurence Valley, N. Y.; married.

II. 14. B. 1851, Nova Scotia. A short, rather stout woman. Has brown eyes and hair, wrinkled skin, no teeth, and most peculiar traits. She is very blunt and outspoken; nervous, excitable and subject to fits of nervous hysterics, when she will cry for days at a time. Is considered mentally lacking by the neighbors; became so peculiar after the menopause that the family feared insanity; is said to have a violent temper. She looks ill and wild and appears almost foolish at times. Has a horror of seeing people; will not open the door. Three visits of the field worker were unsuccessful but on the fourth she was admitted and treated kindly. II, 14 said she had seen the field worker each time, and finally decided it must be something important; the information asked for was given willingly and in a clear concise manner. She married II, 13, b. about 1858, in Nova Scotia, a large very kind man with gray hair and moustache, blue eyes with a cataract, very large nose and the appearance of general moral and mental normality. They have 8 children, III, 11-18.

III. 11. B. 1871, of good repute, married to E. C., a daughter b. 1907, Somerville, Mass.

III. 12. B. 1875. A very short, slender woman, dark-brown hair and eyes, a small thin face. Has tuberculosis of the throat, but has improved in a sanitarium. Is nervous and high strung, but has good control of herself. Married N. B., a Jew, much against her parents' wishes. They live in a good clean apartment. She is a dressmaker, of average intelligence and good repute.

III. 13. B. 1877, G——, d. 1879, measles and lung disease.

III. 14. B. 1879, G——, d. 1884, fell from wharf and was drowned.

III. 15. B. 1884, G——, a very small excitable woman; cries for days at a time. Is now in a sanitarium for *nervous diseases*. Married T. J. a drummer. They have a comfortable home in L.

III. 16. B. 1886, in the town of G——. A small slight, quick, active woman with brown eyes and hair, small face and features. Has always suffered from epileptic fits; but these do not seem to have affected her mentally. It is said she had 14 attacks the day her child was born. She married E. K., twice her age, a tall slight man with very gray hair, gray eyes, thin face, sharp features, who looks ill. They live in a well-kept tenement in a good section.

III. 16. B. 1886, small, slight woman; brown eyes and hair. Epileptic. Quick and active.

III. 17. B. 1890, d. 1892, food did not agree with her.

III. 18. B. 1894, a very large boy about 6 feet tall, weight 197 lbs. Brown eyes and hair. Full, round face, large features, average mentality; electrician, was mixed in an assault on a young girl, but was acquitted.

PATIENT'S MOTHER'S FATHER'S FATHER AND MOTHER.

I. 3. B. 1822, Nova Scotia, drowned at sea, 1882. Married I, 4, b. 1824 Nova Scotia; was subject to epileptic fits, which often succeeded each other rapidly. Was of good repute and preserved her mentality till her death at 80 years of cancer of the stomach.

PATIENT'S MOTHER'S MOTHER AND HER FRATERNITY.

II. 16. B. 1858 Nova Scotia. A tall, heavy woman with light hair, blue eyes, and large face with very hard expression. Dressed very well and lives in a good tenement; is reported to have been sensual and immoral like her daughter and granddaughter (whom she bitterly denounces) and to have been most cruel to her husband.

II. 17. Two males said to have been normal, respectable.

II. 18. Two females of whom little is known.

II. 19. Two females immoral, and one of these feebleminded.

II. 20. Female said to be of good repute.

II. 21. Female died in infancy.
II. 22. Three males of whom nothing is known.
II. 23. Two males died in infancy.

PATIENT'S MOTHER'S MOTHER'S FATHER.

I. 5. B. 1822, Nova Scotia. A man of very bad repute, grossly immoral; is living in Nova Scotia. Has 3 children.

PATIENT'S MOTHER'S MOTHER'S MOTHER.

I. 6. B. 1827, N. S. A woman of bad repute. Is reported to have kept a notorious house in Liverpool, N. S. Her husband was so immoral that she left him and came to Boston. Here she was a nurse for many years and seems to have had a very good reputation for morality. She is described as having been lightheaded, very imaginative, and not always quite responsible.

XII. THE STUDY OF HUMAN HEREDITY*.

Methods of Collecting, Charting and Analyzing Data.

BY DAVENPORT, GODDARD, JOHNSTONE, LAUGHLIN, WEEKS.

The following methods are in use at the Eugenics Record Office at Cold Spring Harbor, Long Island, The New Jersey State Village for Epileptics, at Skillman, and The Training School for Backward and Feeble-Minded Children, at Vineland, New Jersey.

1. THE FIELD WORKER.

For many years the better organized Hospitals and Institutions for defectives have kept family histories of the patients. The information obtained from application blanks, physicians' examinations and replies received from letters sent to relatives and physicians have been compiled and tabulated and deductions have been drawn from them. But it has for some time been apparent that such family histories are far from satisfactory and that a better way to get at the method of inheritance of epilepsy, feeble-mindedness and the various forms of insanity and criminality is by means of a field worker, who goes to the homes and interviews persons that can and will give the desired information.

* Reprinted from Eugenics Record Office: Bulletin No. 2.

Besides the research work, the field worker performs many of the services that usually fall under the head of purely social worker. In many cases patients who have not heard from friends or relatives in years are brightened by the visit of the field worker and look forward to her return in the hope that she may bring them news of their friends. Discharged patients are visited by the field worker whenever possible in order to keep the Institution in touch with them. Her visits to relatives, physicians and others establish a friendly feeling toward, and an intelligent understanding of, the Institution and its work.

When connected with an Institution, the field worker (who for the purposes of many studies is preferably a woman) first learns all she can about the patient from the material at the office, such as correspondence, application blanks, records of medical and psychological examinations. Addresses of friends and relatives and other information that may be helpful in locating them is recorded and put in form for the worker to take with her. Just before starting out to visit the relatives and friends, the field worker visits the patient in his ward or cottage. This is done in the manner of a friendly visit. She learns from the patient all that he or she can tell about the friends and relatives, especially with reference to their addresses, etc. The patients enjoy these visits, and are often able to give very useful information.

Everything now being ready for the visit to the home, the field worker, armed with recent personal knowledge of the patient, which assures her cordial welcome, visits the home and interviews the relatives, friends and family physician. To secure satisfactory results, sympathetic and confidential relations must always be maintained. It is better to leave some details to another visit than to have relations at all strained. The field worker's constant endeavor must be to establish a feeling between the family and Institution that will assure her of a welcome at any time with kindly cooperation, and to this end she sacrifices minor details that would naturally come on return visits. The field worker endeavors to see as many relatives as possible. In this way facts omitted or overlooked by one are often recalled and told in full detail by another, and by this means information already obtained is confirmed. Every additional interview is sure to reveal new facts.

Addresses of relatives who live in other sections are recorded to be used later by an investigator in that section. References to foreign countries are also kept, with the town, and wherever possible, the street address. In the case of foreign born parents, an endeavor is made to obtain data relative to the time of immigration, the town from which they came, and other information that may be useful.

Whenever the field worker learns of any defectives who need Institutional care, their names and addresses are obtained, and filed with the other material. By this means useful information is available when application is made for admission to Institutions.

As collected, the data are carefully recorded, and the pedigree chart made of the family. This is then put in permanent form on a sheet of white paper 8 x 10½ inches, with such notes and symbols as have been adopted to designate certain traits. A full description, with all details, is typewritten and filed with the chart.

2. THE CHART (Plate I).

The plan of charting adopted is based on the decisions of a committee of the American Association for the Study of the Feeble-Minded held at Lincoln, Illinois, in 1910. This committee consisted of Supt. E. R. Johnstone and Dr. H. H. Goddard, of Vineland, N. J.; and Drs. A. C. Rogers, of Faribault, Minn., Wm. Healy of Chicago, Ill., Wm. T. Shanahan of Sonyea, N. Y., and David F. Weeks of Skillman, N. J.

The system is a rectangular one, the symbols for the individuals *(individual symbols)* of a fraternity (full brothers and sisters) being on the same horizontal line, with each later generation placed below the next earlier. Male individuals are indicated by squares, females by circles, suspended by vertical lines *(individual lines)* from the horizontal line. Members of one fraternity are connected by the same horizontal line. The rank of birth in the fraternity is indicated by a serial number placed immediately above the *fraternity line.* When the sex is unknown the square or circle is omitted from the end of the individual line. The fraternity line is connected by a vertical line *(descent line)* to a line joining the symbols of father and mother *(mating line).* The mating line may be a short horizontal one or oblique, passing from one consort to the other as emergencies of space decide. Dotted mating lines are used for illegal unions. When a marriage of one of the individuals of a fraternity who occupies a middle position in the series is to be represented, the consort is placed below and to the right or left of the circle or square and joined to it by an oblique line from which is dropped a *descent line* meeting the fraternity line. In the case of illegitimate children, the descent line is dotted.

For purposes of reference from description to chart each sheet of a pedigree is numbered serially with Arabic numerals. On each sheet the generations are numbered serially at the left margin with Roman numerals (I, II, III, etc.) beginning with the oldest generation. In each generation each individual symbol is numbered with Arabic numerals from left to right. In the text reference is made to an individual on the chart by sheet, generation and individual number. Thus 1, II, 17 means the first sheet, II generation, 17th individual symbol from the left. For the sake of uniformity in charting the families, the paternal side of the family is placed at the left of the chart, the maternal side at the right.

(For display charts. As a matter of convenience and as an aid in tracing the patient's immediate family, showing at a glance the lines of paternal and maternal descent of the defect, the descent line connecting the paternal side may be made green. Red may be used for the lines connecting the individuals on the maternal side. That the patient's symbol may stand out more prominently and make the reading of the chart easier, the fraternity to which he or she belongs may be dropped below the others.)

Besides the lines and individual symbols a nomenclature is used that gives in brief much information for the interpretation of the chart. The following capital letters are used inside or around the individual symbols as follows:

A	alcoholic, decidedly intemperate,	M	migrainous,
B	blind,	N	normal,
C	criminalistic,	Ne	neurotic,
D	deaf,	P	paralytic,
E	epileptic,	S	syphilitic,
F	feeble-minded,	Sx	sexually immoral,
G	gonorrheal,	T	tubercular,
I	insane,	W	vagrant (tramp, confirmed runaway).

An index hand points to the individual whose heredity is being studied.

A line under a symbol indicates that this individual is or has been an inmate of some Institution.

A small black disc at the end of an individual line indicates a still-birth or miscarriage.

When the individual is the subject of several defects or diseases, the additional letters are arranged around the individual symbol. Symbols for traits that are not designated above are written beneath the individual symbol. When no letter accompanies the individual symbol it means that no definite data had been secured at the time the chart was made. The trait—alcoholism, criminality, deafness, epilepsy, feeble-mindedness, insanity, etc.—which the field worker is chiefly studying may be called the primary trait for the chart or pedigree. An individual showing the primary trait is represented by a solid symbol, printed (if desired) in color with the corresponding letter intaglio.[1] These symbols are shown in full size in plate V.

In studies on insanity it is suggested that qualifying lower case letters, used singly or in combination, should, whenever possible, be added to the letter I, e. g.:

a alcoholic insanity,
d dementia præcox,
g general paralysis of the insane,
m manic depressive insanity,
p paranoia,
s senile dementia,
t traumatic insanity.

On the pedigree chart, b stands for born; m, for married; † or d, for dead or died; † (or d) inf. means died at or before two years of age; † (d) young, means died before the age when the trait normally develops or is detectable; e. g., with feeble-mindedness before six years; with epilepsy before fourteen; with insanity before twenty.

In case other traits or causes of death are given on the chart they may be abbreviated as follows:

bd	Bright's disease,	*cc*	eccentricity,
ca	cancer,	*en*	encephalitis,
cb	childbirth,	*go*	goitre,
ch	chorea,	*gp*	general paralysis of the insane.
cr	cripple,		
df	deformed,	*hy*	hysteria,
dp	dementia præcox,	*id*	ill defined organic disease,
dt	delirium tremens,	*kd*	kidney disease,
dy	dropsy,	*la*	locomotor ataxia.

---

[1] Red is being used for epilepsy, green for insanity, violet for criminality, black for feeble-mindedness. When the individual does not show the primary trait or associated secondary trait he is marked "N," but this does not necessarily mean that he is normal in all respects.

md manic depressive insanity,
np neuropathic condition,
obs obesity,
pa paranoia,
pn pneumonia,
sh shiftlessness,
sm simple meningitis,
sb softening of the brain,
sco scoliosis,
sd senile dementia,
su suicide,
va varices, varicose veins,
ve vertigo,
x unknown,
? implies doubt.

When preceded by a † (or d) the term indicates the cause of death.

In making the charts rubber stamps may be used to advantage. Standard sizes of these may be obtained from Lewis F. Walton, 12 South Fourth Street, Philadelphia. Other lettering may be done with a typewriter. (Plates III, IV.)

3. THE DESCRIPTION.

The full description of an individual, as herein contemplated, comprises the following thirteen points. It is obtained for each person in the family so far as practicable.

1. Name (maiden name of all married women; method of spelling surname preferred by the family to be ascertained and used. First time field worker uses a surname in her report it is to be written in Gothic capital letters, e. g., **DE BOW**).

2. Sex, if not sufficiently indicated by name (Frances, Francis; Jessie, Jesse; Marion, Marian; etc., frequently confused).

3. Date of birth. (This gives order of birth, age at time of interview, age at death, if dead, etc. Should be accurate to the month. Useful for reference to town and vital records.)

4. Place of birth. (Tells at least where mother was at given date and probably locates entire family; frequently assists in helping to connect with related families in same general locality; locates town where birth records may be sought.)

5. If dead, date of death or age at death approximatey. (Essential in getting proportions of affected among those who reach the *age of incidence.)*

6. Cause of death. (Get the best diagnosis possible, inquiring of family physician where practicable and learn if any autopsy was performed. So far as possible use the terms employed in "Causes of Sickness and Death," United States Census Bureau, 1910. Field workers should study this list. Note directions given in paragraph

below entitled "Description of Traits and Causes of Sickness and Death.")

7. Place of death. (Useful in comparison with town and vital records.)

8. If immigrant, date of immigration (steamship and port of entry where possible).

9. Mental and physical condition of each person. (Note paragraph, "Description of Traits and Causes of Sickness and Death.")

10. If married, a description with full name of consort, or of consorts, if married more than once; of the children, and of the consort's parents.

11. Occupations, whenever possible.

12. A general description of the home influences, environment and education.

13. For each family, the sources of information. (Names, addresses and relationships of the individual who is being primarily studied.)

Description of Traits and Causes of Sickness and Death. The field worker naturally directs inquiries primarily toward the specific trait that is being studied (herein called *primary* trait). But the opportunity is utilized to learn of other traits that may be significantly or incidentally associated with the primary trait. In describing traits, the person interviewed is encouraged to talk freely while the field worker records the essential points in the description. In the case of the primary traits too much detail can hardly be obtained, and even in the associated traits she is not to be satisfied with vague terms if details can be obtained. N. B. Experience indicate that it is not desirable for the field worker to use a printed form in her interviews.

Such vague terms, to be used only when further details cannot be obtained are: *abscess,* without cause or location; *accident; decline,* without naming disease; *cancer,* without specifying organ first affected; *congestion,* without naming organ affected; *convulsions,* without details and period of life; *fever; heart trouble* and *heart failure; insanity,* without details (when possible distinguish alcoholic psychoses, progressive or general paralysis, senile dementia, softening of the brain, on the one hand, and such forms as manic-depressive insanity, melancholia, paranoia, dementia præcox, on the other) ; *kidney trouble; lung trouble; marasmus; stomach trouble.* The following data are considered especially valuable as symptoms, and should at the judgment of the field worker be made the subject of inquiry: alcoholism.

venereal disease (including gonorrhea and syphilis), sexual immorality, masturbation, St. Vitus' dance or chorea, and sick headaches.

The term "normal" should be used only to indicate that, in respect to the *primary trait,* the individual is believed on trustworthy evidence to be like most people. Normal is not to be applied to persons simply because nothing is known to the contrary.

Limits to Pedigree. How far among collaterals is it desirable to extend the pedigree? This depends on the nature of the primary trait. If, as in the case of most defects, it is due to the absence of a quality essential to normal development then it will be desirable to learn at least of the direct ancestors as far back as possible; the fraternities to which the parents belong; the offspring of all members of such fraternities and the parents of each consort when there are children. Likewise, each of the members of the four grand parental fraternities, their consorts and their children, their children's consorts and the children's children. If the patient has brothers and sisters these together with the patient are studied with the greatest possible care; also their consorts and children, if any.

If the trait is one that never appears in the children unless one parent shows it, then it is desirable to carry back the direct line as far as possible and less attention need be paid to the descendants of certainly normal collaterals beyond what is necessary to establish with certainty the law of inheritance.

4. METHODS OF ANALYSIS.

A brief statement of the Mendelian rules of heredity. So many traits are inherited in accordance with the Mendelian rules that a brief statement of them is appended. But the field worker is warned against being so prejudiced by these rules that her, or his, judgment is warped. The exact facts are to be sought; their interpretation must come later. So far as possible all statements should be verified. In general a statement may be regarded as verified when made by a second, independent witness.

With this caution in mind the Mendelian rules will be found useful in directing the field worker in her inquiries. First, it is important to disabuse the mind of the popular error that traits are inherited from ancestors. Strictly, traits are not inherited at all; what is inherited is a condition of the reproductive or germ cells which determines the development of the trait—the trait depends on the presence or absence of a *determiner* in the germ cells.

Some defects that the field worker will study, such as albinism and feeble-mindedness, are known as recessive defects, i. e., they are defects due to the absence of the determiner making for normality in respect to these traits. Other defects, such as cataract and brachydactylism, are dominant defects, which means that they are due to the presence of some germinal determiner in addition to all the determiners for normality in respect to these characteristics. Thus, in respect to one character there are three gametic and two somatic types of individuals. Somatically, the individual has or has not the defect; these are the two somatic types. Gametically the germ plasm of the individual may possess alternately germ cells with and without the determiner studied; an individual carrying such a germ plasm is said to be *simplex* and somatically cannot be easily distinguished from a *duplex* individual in which every germ cell possesses the determiner in question. The third gametic type is said to be *nulliplex* in which none of the germ cells possess the determiner in question. There are thus six types of gametic matings in reference to a single character; these types may be expressed as follows:

Type 1. $(D + D) \times (D + D) = 4\,DD$
" 2. $(D + D) \times (D + R) = 2\,DD + 2\,DR$
" 3. $(D + D) \times (R + R) = 4\,DR$
" 4. $(D + R) \times (D + R) = DD + 2\,DR + RR$
" 5. $(D + D) \times (R + R) = 2\,DR + 2\,RR$
" 6. $(R + R) \times (R + R) = 4\,RR$

D stands for the determiner for the trait studied and R stands for its absence.

The field worker must understand that research, seeking to unravel the laws of inheritance must work out the gametic nature of each individual studied, hence the necessity of extending the pedigree to all ancestors with collaterals, descendants and consorts of all individuals the make-up of whose germ plasm it is desired to understand. For example, by hypothesis, feeble-mindedness is for the most part a recessive trait and the hypothesis must be tested as follows: The field worker finds a person suffering from feeble-mindedness, a descendant of two normal parents—by hypothesis both of these parents are *simplex;* the field worker must understand that each parent will probably have somewhere in his or her ancestry a feeble-minded person and it is the business of the field worker to make a special search for such person or persons in the pedigree.

Criticism of an actual pedigree reported by a field worker. (Plate II.) This study begins with the epileptic boy III—7. The principal thing, of course, is to describe accurately all of the brothers and sisters of the affected person, they, being produced by the union of the same two germ plasms, will throw light on the make-up of such germ plasm. The pedigree is to be criticised from this standpoint. More information should be got concerning III—6, 8 and 9. The field worker at once notes that the mating II—5 and 6 is the most important one to be studied in that this mating produced the fraternity just described. The father, described as feeble-minded, should form the basis of an extended study. It is noted that his parents died at an old age but nothing further is known of either of them. If possible, they should be proven to be either normal or nervously affected. If normal, then it will be a profitable expenditure of time to search the ancestry and complete fraternities of each for affected individuals, in order thoroughly to test the hypothesis in this mating. Likewise the mating I—1 and 2 should be studied with a view to determining the nature of I—2; it is apparent that if I—2 is normal all of his five children should also be normal, and if they were so it would not be profitable to spend very much time in tracing further his blood. The fraternities II—1 to 5 and II—6 to 12 should be more thoroughly studied in that a detailed knowledge of each will throw light on the nature of the germ plasm producing II—5 and 6. More should also be known concerning the consort of II—7 and her "blood," inasmuch as this mating was productive of abnormal offspring. The other consorts of the II generation are not so important, if on investigation the offspring prove all to be normal. Likewise the consorts of III are not so important because their children are all very young; however, for study a few years hence it would be highly desirable to have these persons accurately described, and such description should be made if the requisite information can be secured without too great an expenditure of time.

In this pedigree the field worker has charted the males to the right and the females to the left; this should be reversed for the sake of uniformity of practice. Indicate the year of birth on the pedigree only in the case of young children. This pedigree contains few persons marked (N), normal. It is highly desirable that every person studied should be so thoroughly described that he or she can either be safely marked (N) or given a proper mark designating the type of abnormality possessed.

Appendix 1.

Forms for written Description of the Chart.

A.

Name   No.

Date

Source of information.
    a. name. b. relation to patient. c. address.

The patient and his home.
    a. Description of the patient.
    b. Neighborhood.—good, fair, bad.
    c. Housing.—tenement, separate house, number of rooms used, condition.
    d. Home treatment.—good, bad, fair, neglected.
    e. Number in the household.—adults, number normal, number defective; children, number normal, number defective; number of boarders.
    f. Financial condition.—good, moderate, poor, very poor.
    g. Education.—time in school, grade attended, reason for leaving.

A description of the individuals on the chart, covering the points mentioned in the text (pages 90 and 91), is written up under the following headings:

The patient's fraternity.
The patient's father and his fraternity.
The patient's father's parents and their fraternities.
The patient's mother and her fraternity.
The patient's mother's parents and their fraternities.

B.

Suggested in the case of extended pedigrees, particularly those made independently of institutions.

General statement relating to locality (exact position, topography, density of population and, in rural localities, adaptability to agriculture), housing, social condition, and origin.

Order of personal descriptions. Begin with earliest generation, describe father, mother and all their children. Take the oldest married child (at left hand end of fraternity) describe his consort and their progeny. Next describe their oldest married child, his or her consort and progeny and so on, to the youngest generation. Then return to the next married sib of the next to the youngest fraternity already described, and give an account of his consort and their children, and so continue, working from left to right until all fraternities have been described. For example, in Plate I the following order is followed: I, 1, 2, 3, II 1, 2, 3, II (2), 7, III 1; II (3), 4, III 2, 3, 4, 5, 6, 7, 8. I 4, 5, II (4) 5, 6.

PLATE I.

Example of a simple pedigree chart.

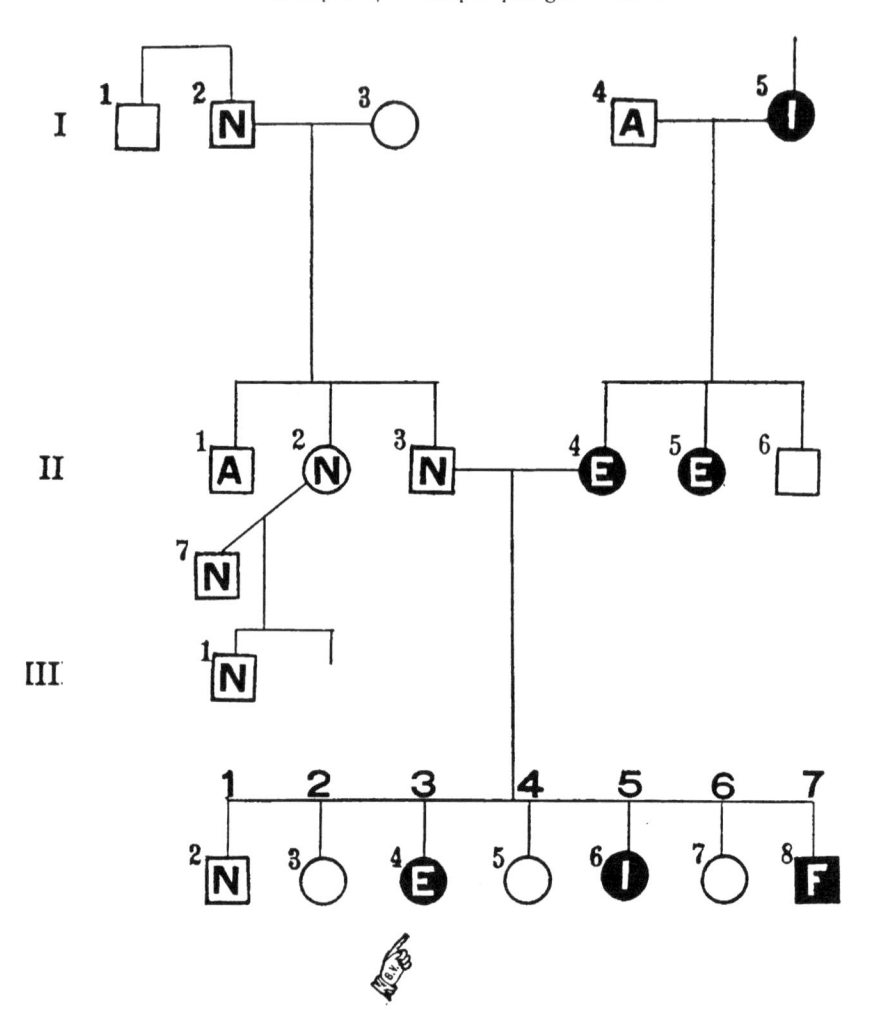

THE FAMILY-HISTORY BOOK.   97

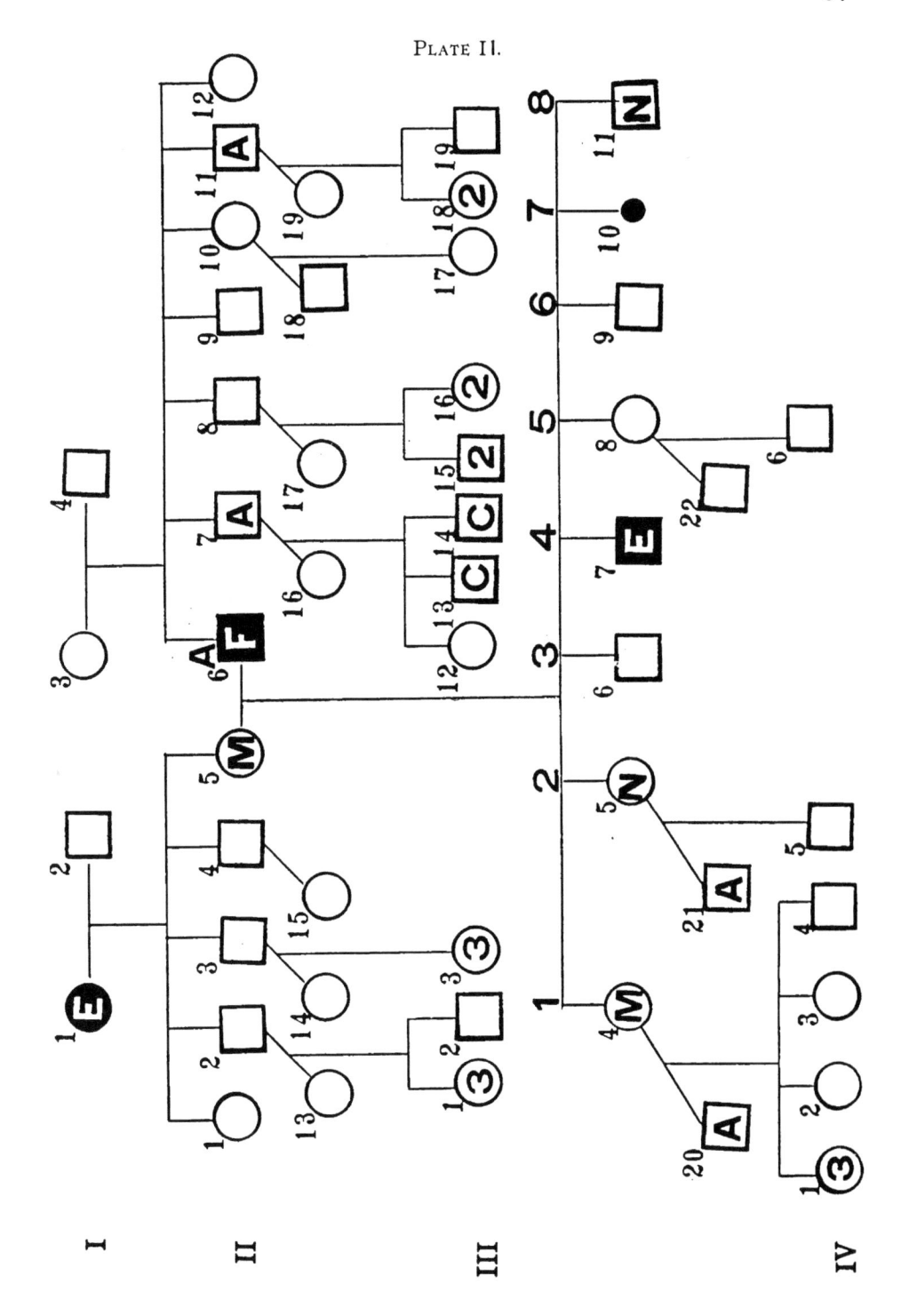

PLATE II.

PLATE III.

Hypothetical pedigree, illustrating use of symbols.

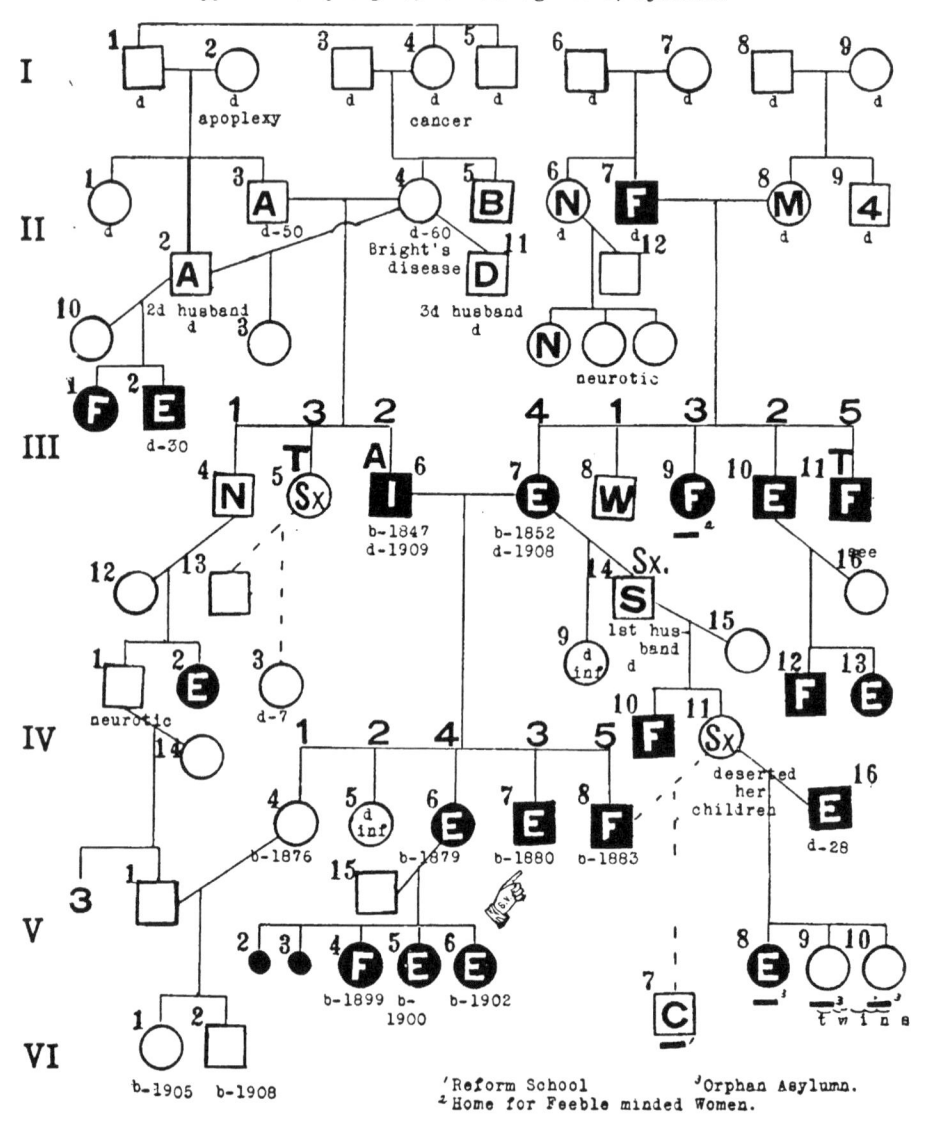

¹ Reform School
² Home for Feeble minded Women.
³ Orphan Asylum.

THE FAMILY-HISTORY BOOK. 99

PLATE IV.

Hypothetical pedigree, illustrating use of symbols.

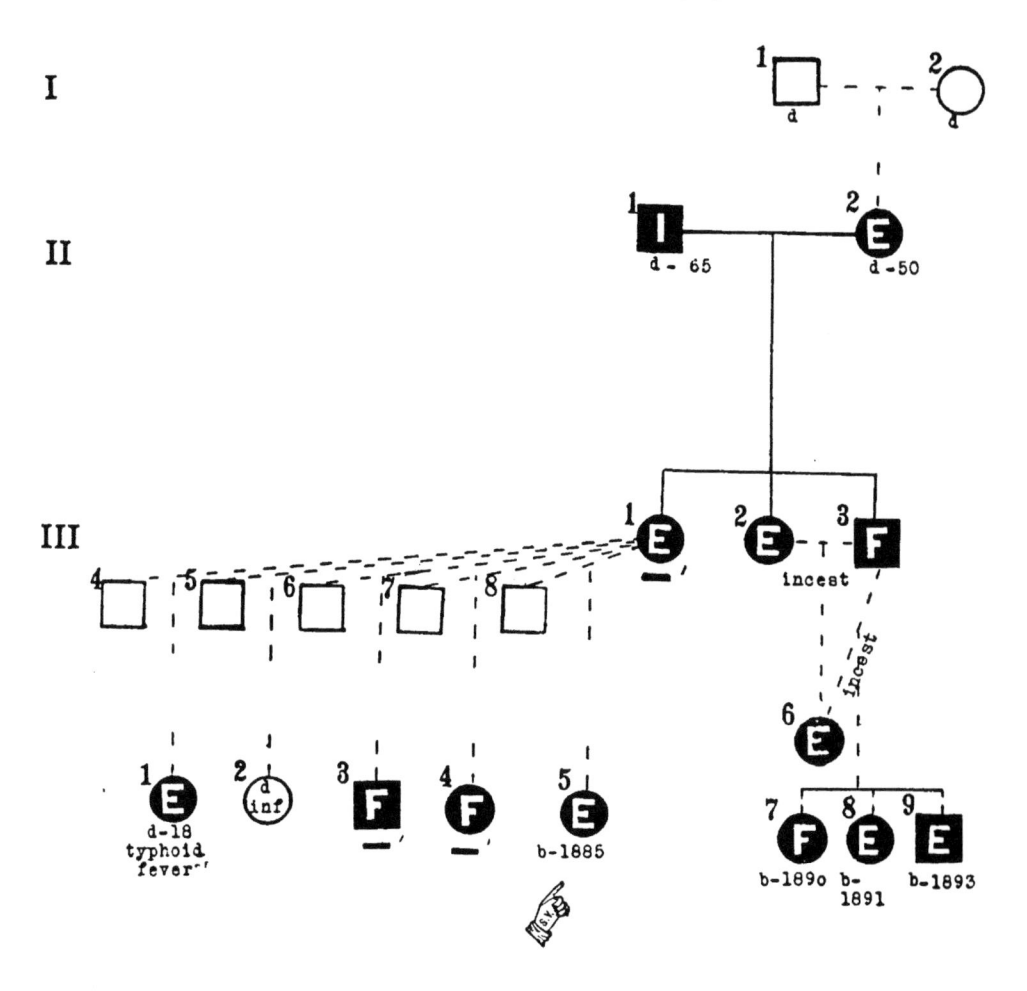

Alms House.

PLATE V.
KEY TO HEREDITY CHART.

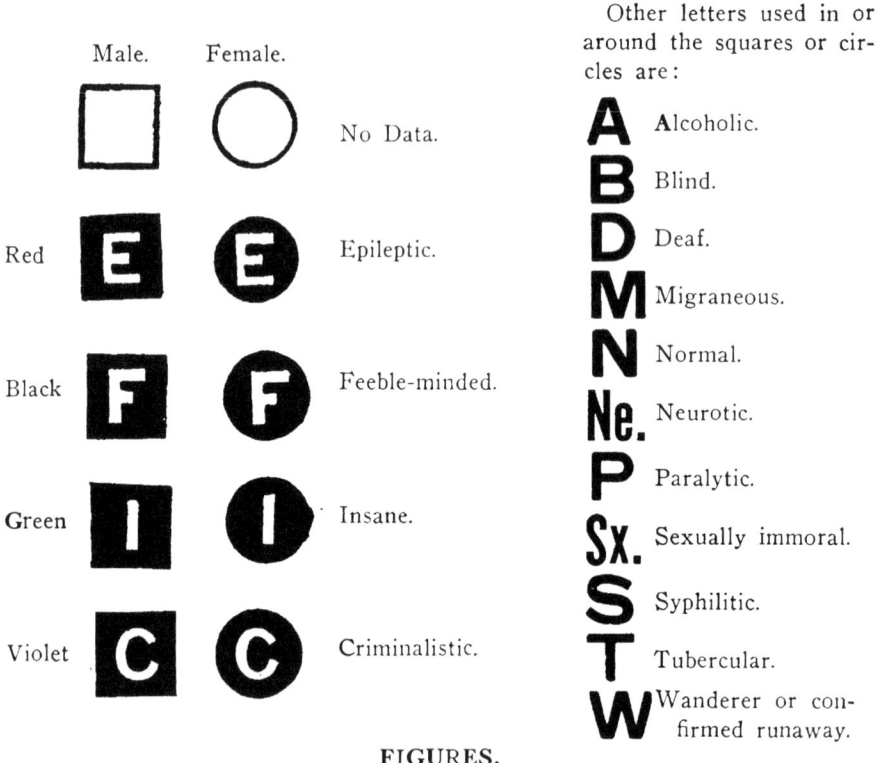

	Male.	Female.		Other letters used in or around the squares or circles are:	
	□	○	No Data.	**A**	**A**lcoholic.
				B	**B**lind.
Red	**E**	**E**	Epileptic.	**D**	**D**eaf.
				M	**M**igraneous.
				N	**N**ormal.
Black	**F**	**F**	Feeble-minded.	**Ne.**	**Ne**urotic.
				P	**P**aralytic.
Green	**I**	**I**	Insane.	**Sx.**	**S**e**x**ually immoral.
				S	**S**yphilitic.
Violet	**C**	**C**	Criminalistic.	**T**	**T**ubercular.
				W	**W**anderer or confirmed runaway.

FIGURES.
Above the line—Order in the line of birth.
    Above the square or circle—Individual reference number.
    Below the square or circle—Age at time of death or date of birth or death.
    In squares or circles—Number of individuals of that sex.

SMALL LETTERS.
b—Born.   † or (d)—Died or dead.
† (d) inf.—Died in infancy.   m—Married.

LINES.
Solid—Connects married individuals and fraternities.
Dotted—Not married or illegitimate.
For display charts.
    Green—Paternal side ⎫ of individual under study.
    Red—Maternal side ⎭
    Violet—Connects related charts or individuals on more than one chart.

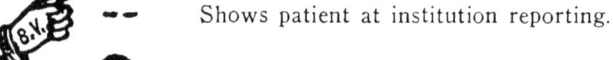

SYMBOLS.
    Shows patient at institution reporting.

    Miscarriage or stillbirth.

    Institutional care (place under symbol).

Plate VI.

SYNOPSIS OF ABBREVIATIONS ADOPTED.

To be used with full face symbols.

▮a, alcoholic insanity.

▮d, dementia precox.

▮g, general paralysis of the insane.

▮m, manic depressive insanity.

▮p, paranoia.

▮s, senile dementia.

▮t, traumatic insanity.

To be written on chart.

bd	Bright's disease.	*la*	locomotor ataxia.
ca	cancer.	*md*	manic depressive insanity.
cb	childbirth.	*np*	neuropathic condition.
ch	chorea.	*obs*	obesity.
cr	cripple.	*pa*	paranoia.
df	deformed.	*pn*	pneumonia.
dp	dementia precox.	*sh*	shiftlessness.
dt	delirium tremens.	*sm*	simple meningitis.
dy	dropsy.	*sb*	softening of the brain.
cc	eccentricity.	*sco*	scoliosis.
en	encephalitis.	*sd*	senile dementia.
go	goitre.	*su*	suicide.
gp	general paralysis of the insane.	*va*	varices, varicose veins.
hy	hysteria.	*ve*	vertigo.
id	ill-defined organic disease.	*x*	unknown.
kd	kidney disease.	*?*	implies doubt.

American Breeders' Association—Eugenics Section

E. E. SOUTHARD, Chairman.   C. B. DAVENPORT, Secretary

The Eugenics Record Office

Cold Spring Harbor, Long Island, N. Y.

ESTABLISHED in October, 1910, this office aims to fill the need of a clearing house for data concerning "blood lines" and family traits in America. It is accumulating and studying records of mental and physical characteristics of human families to the end that the people may be better advised as to fit and unfit matings. It issues blank schedules (sent on application) for the use of those who wish to preserve a record of their family histories.

The Eugenics Section and its Record Office are a development from the former committee on Eugenics, comprising well-known students of heredity and humanists; among others Alexander Graham Bell, Washington, D. C.; Luther Burbank, Santa Rosa, Cal.; W. E. Castle, Harvard University; C. R. Henderson, University of Chicago; Adolf Meyer, Johns Hopkins University; J. Arthur Thomson, University of Aberdeen; H. J. Webber, Cornell University; Frederick A. Woods, Harvard Medical School. The work of the Record Office is aided by the advice of a number of technical committees. Its superintendent is H. H. Laughlin, Cold Spring Harbor, N. Y., to whom correspondence may be addressed.

PUBLICATIONS

Bulletin No. 1. Heredity of Feeblemindedness. H. H. Goddard, April, 1911. 10 cents.

Bulletin No. 2. The Study of Human Heredity. C. B. Davenport, H. H. Laughlin, David F. Weeks, E. R. Johnstone, Henry H. Goddard, May, 1911. 10 cents.

Bulletin No. 3. Preliminary Report of a Study of Heredity in Insanity in the Light of the Mendelian Laws. Gertrude L. Cannon and A. J. Rosanoff, May, 1911. 10 cents.

Bulletin No. 4. A First Study of Inheritance in Epilepsy. C. B. Davenport and David F. Weeks, November, 1911. 15 cents.

Bulletin No. 5. A Study of Heredity of Insanity in the Light of the Mendelian Theory. A. J. Rosanoff and Florence I. Orr, November, 1911. 10 cents.

Bulletin No. 6. The Trait Book. C. B. Davenport, February, 1912. 10 cents.

Memoir No. 1. The Hill Folk. Report on a Rural Community of Hereditary Defectives. Florence H. Danielson and Charles B. Davenport, August, 1912. 75 cents.

Memoir No. 2. The Nam Family. A Study in Cacogenics. Arthur H. Estabrook and Charles B. Davenport, September, 1912. $1.00.

Record of Family Traits. Free.

UNIVERSITY OF CALIFORNIA LIBRARY
This book is DUE on the last date stamped below.

OCT 16 1947

JUN 10 1991

SENT ON ILL

APR 1 8 1997

U.C. BERKELEY

22May62HH

MAY 8 1962

8 Feb'64JE   APR 2 5 2006 -9 PM

REC'D LD

2 5 '64 -11 AM

-100m-12,'46(A2012s16)4120